SYRIAN CHRISTIANS IN MUSLIM SOCIETY

*Princeton Studies on the Near East*

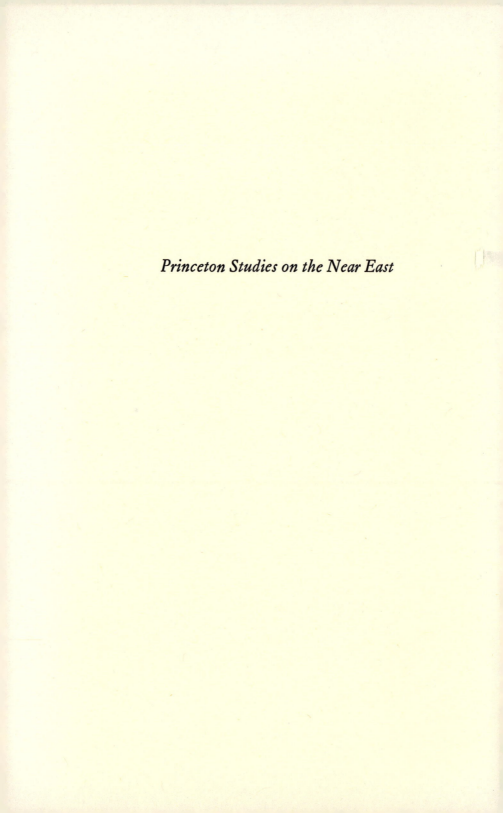

# Syrian Christians in Muslim Society

## AN INTERPRETATION

*by* ROBERT M. HADDAD

Princeton University Press, Princeton, New Jersey

1970

*L.C. Card: 75-113002*
*ISBN 0-691-03086-3*

This book has been composed in Linotype Granjon

*Publication of this book has been supported by Smith College, by the Department of Near Eastern Studies of Princeton University, and by the Louis A. Robb Fund of Princeton University Press.*

Printed in the United States of America
by Princeton University Press, Princeton, New Jersey

*For*

*Hadbo Trabulsi Haddad*

*and to the memory of*

*Nadra Abdo Haddad*

لا زار جفني الكرى لا هزّني الطربُ

ان كنتُ يومًا لغير العرب أنتسبُ

لندره عبده حدّاد

# ACKNOWLEDGMENTS

RESEARCH for this essay was assisted by a grant awarded by the Joint Committee on the Near and Middle East of the Social Science Research Council and the American Council of Learned Societies, and by a supplementary grant awarded by the Committee on Aid to Faculty Scholarship of Smith College. This latter Committee also provided a generous publication grant, the necessity for which must make the judicious grieve. Additional support toward the same end was provided by the Department of Near Eastern Studies of Princeton University, and by the Louis A. Robb Fund of Princeton University Press.

I should like to acknowledge the courtesy extended by the Public Record Office in London, the Archives Nationales in Paris and, especially, the Archives of the Sacred Congregation for the Propagation of the Faith in Rome. Mīkhā'īl Burayk's work on the Patriarchs of Antioch, which is Manuscript 14 in the Bibliothèque Orientale de Beyrouth, was reproduced for me by the Bibliothèque Orientale through the mediation of Professor Yusuf Ibish of the American University of Beirut. I am duly grateful. Some years ago the Vatican Library provided me with a microfilm of a portion of Macarius al-Za'īm's chronology of the Patriarchs of Antioch and it is a pleasant duty publicly to acknowledge, however belatedly, that assistance.

Professor Richard N. Verdery of McGill University saw this essay in embryonic form and gave encouragement; Professor L. Carl Brown of Princeton University read the completed manuscript and helped launch it toward publication. They too have my thanks. Mrs. A. B. McArthur typed and read proof with her customary patience and sure intelligence. William A., Emily, Leila and both Josettes helped. So too did my wife Helen, of all editors the loveliest and best.

Wendell, Massachusetts
July 17, 1970

# CONTENTS

# ABBREVIATIONS

## USED FOR CERTAIN ARCHIVAL MATERIAL

| | |
|---|---|
| Arch. Prop. | L'Archivio della S. Congregazione di Propaganda Fide<br>*SOCG* Le Scritture originali riferite nelle Congregazioni Generali<br>*SC* Scritture riferite nei Congressi<br>*CP* Congregazioni Particolari |
| A. E. | France. Archives Nationales. *Ministère des Affaires Étrangères* |
| S. P. | Great Britain. Public Record Office. *State Papers* |

SYRIAN CHRISTIANS IN MUSLIM SOCIETY

# *SYRIAN CHRISTIANS IN MUSLIM SOCIETY*

## AN INTERPRETATION

ON THE politically dominant community whose institutions are more or less formed and stable, the marginal community can have little effect. The latter's power to influence and shape is greatest at those junctures when the characteristic institutions of the dominant community are in the process of formation, radical modification, or destruction by forces which the marginal community may or may not have helped generate but which it is able to accelerate and focus. Twice the Syrian Christians (marginal by virtue of Muslim definition sustained by Muslim political power) have played this role, each time by accelerating the movement of profane learning from the "West" to the Islamic world; on the first occasion conducting, in part through their Christianity and in part through the Greek learning they had assimilated to their faith, many of the intellectual currents which were to lead to the creation of the salient institutions of Islamic civilization; and on the second occasion, a millennium later, accelerating through the thrust of their own aspirations, aroused and instructed by their earlier and more intimate connections with European civilization, a number of those forces which were to modify radically, when they did not destroy, the characteristic institutions of the dominant Arab Muslim community.

Substantively, of course, the cultural role of the numerically preponderant Syrian Christians in the early Islamic centuries and that of the Arabized Syrian Christian minorities in the modern era differed as much as the distinct epochs in which each group labored. There exists nonetheless an organic connection between the early and later process, since each was rooted in an epoch which demanded radical institutional change within Muslim society and so afforded the marginal Christians the opportunity to influence the self-definition of the dominant community. Obviously, however, the concrete results of each process were not analogous. The earlier was instrumental in the construction of a religiously rationalized non-Christian society, and the part played by Syrian Christians in that development could extend little beyond transmission—that is, they posed many of the critical questions and provided much of the material and method with which Islam would frame its own answers to those questions.

This first age of transmission closed when, somewhat before the end of the great formative phase of Islamic civilization, its appointed task was done. There emerged then those definitions by which the dominant community would abide and, abiding, push further toward the margin all those who refused fully to accept them. And under the prolonged disability which is its fate, the marginal community—even if still a numerical majority—necessarily turns inward, closes upon itself; the creative urge withers and the cultural achievement becomes confined largely to preservation and commentary on that preserved.

Thus the ever more emphatic marginality of the Syrian Christians after the formative phase of Islamic civilization served progressively to deplete their resources, intellectual and artistic no less than human and material.

Yet if the Islamic centuries worked to erode the energies and resources of the Christians, Islamic tolerance served virtually to ensure Christian survival. Survival ensured, in turn, that any opportunity—short of conversion—which seemed to promise the Christians an end to marginality would be seized upon by the more aware and ambitious among them. But this opportunity comes in its fullness only when the characteristic institutions of the dominant community evidence failing viability, when survival of the dominant community seems to necessitate new institutional expression, new definitions. So in modern times, as the Western assault demonstrated the inadequacy of traditional Islamic institutions, the Syrian Christians, because of their earlier exposure to the West and their understandably greater receptivity to its various messages, assumed once more the transmitter's role.

This second age of transmission, however, was, in the motivation of its movers and in its effect, markedly different from the first. For on the second occasion, and however unconsciously, the Syrian Christians strove for the dissolution of an Islamic order which, if true to its own canons, could only affirm for Christians that marginal status which had been theirs for over a thousand years. Hence the effort of Syrian Christians in the late nineteenth and twentieth century to create essentially secular nationalisms which would be blind to confessional distinctions or, as in the case of Lebanese nationalism, would even incline toward Christian predominance. In this period the transmitter tended to metamorphose into the innovator, the would-be definer of the new.

The Syrian Christians' modern contact with the West began, of course, in the Ottoman era, an era which saw, as it unfolded, fundamental changes taking place within these Christian communities, changes whereby they acquired the knowledge and awareness and clarified those aspirations which would enable them once more to don the transmitter's mantle, this time in the eastern Arab world of late and post-Ottoman times. The events of the Ottoman era, therefore, will command the burden of this essay's historical analysis, for it was the period wherein a world was undone and another promised, one which gave the Syrian Christians a glimpse of new possibilities. The age of the Osmanli may be seen as the preparatory phase for the second age of transmission.

The primary concerns of this essay then are three: to indicate in broad outline the nature of Syrian Christian participation in the formative phase of Islamic civilization; to describe and analyze in some detail the alterations in the condition and prospects of the Syrian Christians —notably the Maronites and Melkites (Orthodox and, after c. 1650, Uniate as well)—during the disintegrative phase of Ottoman Islamic civilization; and, reverting once more to the broad stroke, to clarify the distinct parts played by the Syrian Christian communities as Ottoman collapse seemed to compel the eastern Arab world to develop non-Islamic norms of political and social organization.

## I

A DIFFICULT geography, generally less favorable to the administrator than to the outlaw and heretic, together with the ideas of men moving in trade and conquest from the Persian plateau and Anatolia, Egypt and Arabia, Greece and Rome, have been the historic guarantors of Syrian religious diversity.

The unity of Christianity in its birthplace scarcely survived the conversion of Constantine by a hundred years. The Islamic faith carried by the invading Arabs in the seventh century encountered a Syrian Christianity decisively and disastrously fractured by those religio-social movements of the fifth century known as the "christological controversies." Directed as much against Byzantine imperial control as against Byzantine religious orthodoxy, these controversies provided Orthodox Christendom with two of its most enduring heresies—the Nestorian and Monophysite (the Syrian adherents of this latter commonly known then as now as "Jacobites"). Energetic Byzantine efforts at reconciliation in the late sixth and early seventh century, in advancing yet another definition of the nature of Christ, produced only further fragmentation. The resultant Monothelite heresy, however, was largely eliminated during the Crusades when most of its erstwhile adherents, the Maronites, submitted to Rome and were joined soon after by their more recalcitrant fellows. Maronite submission to the papal see represented perhaps the most important legacy, at least on Syrian soil, of the Western Christian intrusion. In any event the Maronites have since remained, though with varying degrees of enthusiasm, committed to Rome.

It is likely that the Muslim conquest found the largely rural-based Jacobites numerically preponderant. The Orthodox Melkites ("Royalists") for their part, while represented in rural Syria, enjoyed greatest strength in the cities where Byzantine government and culture had been most vital. The Nestorians, their areas of greatest concentration being Mesopotamia and Persia, were of no great importance in geographic Syria.[1] The then Monothelite Maronites[2] were a fledgling and still largely monastic community whose evolution into one of the two most important Syrian Christian sects was to await migration to, and centuries of residence in, the mountain refuge of the Lebanon.

Inevitably, Islam exacted a heavy toll. Yet it must be emphasized that the process of apostasy, though relentless, was nevertheless gradual. No attempt was made by any Muslim government to exterminate the Christians, and only rare and isolated attempts were made forcibly to convert them. They were, by Koranic designation, "People of the Book"—men who possessed, albeit in incomplete and perverted form, Divine revelation—and as such were granted wide internal autonomy under their own ecclesiastical leaders and law. In return, they were to submit to the temporal authority of the Muslim state, pay a special poll tax, and endure certain legal and social disabilities. If, on one hand, the considerable autonomy granted tended to preserve the various Christian sects, their marginal status could effect ultimately only their cultural and numerical impoverishment. At few times in the course of the Muslim centuries was it other than perfectly clear to the non-Muslim that most mundane interests would be served by conversion to the faith of the Prophet. Only

[1] By "geographic Syria" is meant that territory delimited by the Taurus Range, Sinai, the Mediterranean, and the Syrian Desert.

[2] One is, of course, aware of the Maronites' insistence upon their "perpetual orthodoxy."

apostasy offered the full range of possibility. Most non-Muslims were to take that step.

The reduction of the Nestorians and Jacobites was most complete—and not entirely for the preceding reasons. Their heavily rural concentration in the east not only exposed the Nestorians to the perennial pressures of Arab nomads (which pressures increased always in direct proportion to the weakness of the central government) but placed them squarely in the path of the Turkomen and Mongol invasions of the eleventh, twelfth, and thirteenth centuries. Nor was their plight alleviated by the Timurid "restoration." The Jacobites, concentrated in the rural east and west, were exposed to many of the same pressures of Arab and Turkomen tribes as well as to maximum damage from the general economic decline and relative intolerance (this latter largely a Crusader legacy) of the Mamlūk period, c. 1250-1516. With these factors must be noted the lack of moral and material support from cosectaries beyond the "Abode of Islam." The only other Monophysites in any number were the Copts of Egypt and perhaps the Armenians[3]—the former under the sway of Islam and undergoing the same process of erosion as their Syrian brethren, while the free development of the latter was threatened now by Byzantium and now by Islam. The far-flung missionary activity of the Nestorians, and to some extent the Jacobites, gave rise only to small, beleaguered, and, excepting the Monophysites of south In-

[3] The Monophysite label is rejected by many Armenians. For our purposes, however, it is their apartness rather than the basis of it which is the important fact.

dia, ultimately ephemeral communities. Nor would any explanation of the almost total reduction of the Nestorians and Jacobites be complete without pointing out that their role (partly the result of the Islamic thrust of their respective christologies?) in the construction of medieval Muslim civilization was of a magnitude sufficient to lead many of them to complete identification with it.

The Maronites were preserved in some strength only by the relative security of their mountain home, for between the exit of the Crusaders and the seventeenth century any support they received from their Latin coreligionists was inconsequential. The Melkites too survived in some strength, essentially because of their urban concentration and their connections with the living and long-creative civilization of Byzantium. For both communities, however, the Mamlūk era was less than happy.

In brief, then, as we approach the sixteenth century and the era of Ottoman Muslim control in Syria, the dominant Christian communities are the Maronites, found almost entirely in the northern sections of Mt. Lebanon, and the Orthodox Melkites, found in small pockets throughout Syria but in strength only in the lower reaches of the mountains above Tripoli and in the urban centers; even in the urban centers, however, they constitute a minority. The Jacobites and Nestorians are numerically insignificant remnants of once proud traditions while a small though economically important Armenian community, ethnically and linguistically distinct from the rest of the Syrian population, can be found mainly in Aleppo. Together, in roughly equal proportions, the Maronites and Melkites make up perhaps one-fourth to one-third of the Syrian population.[4]

[4] This estimate is of course only an informed guess.

## II

As THE seventeenth century opened, and with it the modern history of the Near East, a role for the Syrian Christians in any political or intellectual movement which might fructify in the life of the Muslim community seemed unlikely. Despite the probability that until the late thirteenth century they had formed the majority element in Syrian society, their energies, particularly after the tenth century, had been expended in a struggle for simple survival against a militant faith which was not less successful for substituting a policy of tolerance and studied humiliation for one of open persecution.

At the risk of imposing a rather too neat order on things, it may be claimed that the intellectually and, to a marked degree, aesthetically creative phase of Syrian Christianity ended soon after the demise of the Umayyad Caliphate in 750. The less than one hundred years of this *Arab* Muslim monarchy witnessed the rapid development of the political organization but little more than the first stirrings toward concrete institutionalization of the Islamic theocracy implied by the Koran and the Prophet's community at Madīnah. The still poorly equipped Muslim jurists and theologians could only begin to ponder the questions being posed by Eastern Christianity and the Hellenistic thought it had in part embodied. The intellectual and social milieu was, if anything, more latitudinarian than it had been under the official Orthodoxy of Byzantium and possibly more latitudinarian than at any time until the period following the First World War. So far indeed was the Muslim community from achieving its intellectually distinct identity that the last of the great

Syrian Christian doctors, St. John of Damascus (d. 748) could regard Islam more or less as another Christian heresy.[5] And a certain symbolic richness lies in the fact that the Umayyad dynasty and the Melkite Damascene (who before taking the monk's garb had been, or so legend informs us, friend and drinking companion of the son and heir of the first Umayyad)[6] died within two years of each other. For the destruction of the Umayyads signaled an acceleration of the process of institutionalization of the theoretic Islamic theocracy, and the passing of Syrian Christianity from its creative age to a twilight age of transmission.

This, the first age of transmission, covered the period from roughly 750 to 950 when largely Nestorian and Jacobite translators, working from Greek into Arabic directly or, more commonly, through extant translations in their native Syriac, brought to the eager Muslims virtually the entire range of Syrian Christian and pagan Greek thought, the catalytic agents through which were created the characteristic institutions of medieval Islam. Before the end of the tenth century the law (in Schacht's felicitous phrase, "the essential kernel of Islam")[7] had been shaped in its fullness and theoretic immutability. At the death of al-Ghazzālī in 1111, Islamic law, theology, and mysticism had been launched toward something resembling equilib-

[5] S. Joannes Damascenus, *De Haeresibus Liber*, in Vol. 47 of *Patrologiae Cursus Completus* (Series graeca), ed. J.-P. Migne (81 vols.; Paris, 1856-67), cols. 407-12.

[6] P. K. Hitti, *History of the Arabs* (8th ed.; New York, 1963), p. 246.

[7] Joseph Schacht, "Pre-Islamic Background and Early Development of Jurisprudence," *Law in the Middle East*, ed. M. Khadduri and H. Liebesny (Washington, D.C., 1955), I, 28.

rium, and a self-contained intellectual system more or less definitively formed. Islam, with a brilliance that still impresses, had delineated the area that would contain all journeys. With fewer and fewer exceptions, meaningful political and cultural participation in the life of the Islamic world came to presuppose adherence to the faith of the Prophet in its Sunnī formulation.

The end of the first age of transmission, then, saw the intellectual and aesthetic impulse of the Syrian Christians gradually reduced to commentary and compilation (and these only irregularly pursued), even as their numerical preponderance was reduced from a substantial majority in the eleventh, and even as late as the thirteenth, century to perhaps some 30 percent of the population in the sixteenth.[8] The sustained play of the creative impulse is not characteristic of the beleaguered community. For the Christians who remained, communal preservation was all.

As we have seen, the Nestorians and Jacobites—the principal channels of transmission between Syrian Christian and Hellenistic thought and Islam—were also the most exposed geographically and culturally. And when in 1516 Selīm the Inexorable inaugurated Ottoman rule in Syria, the Christian standard had passed from the Nestorians and Jacobites to the Maronites and Orthodox Melkites. The participation of either community in the emergence of classical Muslim civilization had been of limited scale. If their situation in the Lebanon ensured the survival of the Maronites, it also ensured a marked degree of cultural

[8] Salibi is probably correct in maintaining that "until the late thirteenth century, a vast proportion of the Syrian population was still Christian . . ." (K. S. Salibi, *The Modern History of Lebanon* [London, 1965], p. xvii).

isolation. The Melkites, on the other hand, by virtue of their concentration in geographic Syria, were largely isolated from the great centers of cultural activity in Iraq and Persia. They were, moreover, of all Christians the most suspect by the Muslim temporal authority. This, obviously, because of their natural affinity for the Orthodox Byzantines who, until the fall of Constantinople in 1453, bore the burden of Christendom's effort against Islam. Episodes such as the Byzantine reoccupation of northern Syria from 969 to 1085 served only to deepen the hostility of Islam toward the Orthodox in their midst. This sentiment was not appreciably mitigated by general Melkite hostility to the Crusader presence (c. 1100-1250), for in the aftermath the Syrian Muslims and their Mamlūk governors (c. 1250-1516) did not always distinguish between those in and those not in communion with Rome. In addition, of course, the Muslim attitude was still governed in large measure by Islam's historic struggle against Orthodox Byzantium.

## III

THE SEEDS of the second age of transmission and the new institutional arrangements it helped materially to foster are to be located in the general adoption of Arabic—first as the vernacular tongue and then as the sole literary vehicle—by the Syrian Christians. For the myriads who entered Islam, adoption of Arabic on both levels came rapidly. It was Arabic, after all, in which the final Revelation was framed and the bulk of Islamic learning enshrined. Not unnaturally the linguistic Arabization of those Syrians who clung to their ancestral faith followed substantially different lines.

It would appear that, before the advent of the Crusader, the majority of Syrian Christians had abandoned their native Syriac for the Arabic vernacular. And although Syriac liturgies were retained by the four Syrian Churches, the displacement of Syriac by Arabic in Christian writings continued apace, until, by the early fourteenth century, the Syriac literary tradition was for all significant purposes dead.[9] The Melkites must have differed from the three other Churches principally in their greater exposure to, and partial assimilation of, the Greek ecclesiastical literature emanating from Byzantine sources.[10] But the high Arabic literary culture—which had once embraced even ecclesiastical literature and which, through and somewhat

[9] Although it is impossible at present to indicate precisely when Syriac ceased to be the vernacular of most Syrian Christians, it is reasonably clear that the ninth and tenth centuries saw a rapid decline in the use of Syriac and that, by the eleventh century, Arabic was both in speech and writing dominant. The prolific Syriac production of Bār Hebraeus (Abū al-Faraj), 1226-86, must be considered the climax of Jacobite literature. The Nestorians, for their part, managed to sustain the tradition a generation beyond. For a sound recent summary of the topic see R. A. Bowman, "Syriac Language and Literature," *Encyclopedia Americana*, 1968 ed., Vol. 26, pp. 195-96.

[10] Though doubtless an exaggeration to hold with Karalevskij that Melkite literature during the twelfth and thirteenth centuries was almost entirely a matter of translation from Greek into Arabic (C. Karalevskij, "Antioche," *Dictionnaire d'Histoire et de Géographie Ecclésiastiques*, III, col. 621 [hereafter cited as *DHGE*]), there can be no denying the pervasiveness of Greek ecclesiastical literature from earliest times through today, with perhaps a slight pause during the Mamlūk period when the influence of the see of Constantinople was minimal (see *below*, pp. 21-22).

beyond the first age of transmission, had occupied an honorable, if circumscribed, place alongside the Syriac and Greek[11]—was not to be effectively revived among Syrian Christians until relatively modern times. Although Arabic continued its inroads at the expense of Syriac, at the time of the Ottoman conquest the Syrian Christian clergy (then and until the nineteenth century virtually the sole repository of their communities' learning) could lay claim to only the slightest proficiency in literary Arabic, their few modest productions in the language of the *ḍāḍ* betraying invariably the grossest colloquialisms as well as a decidedly limited intellectual range.[12] The tongue

[11] The great luminary here is of course Theodore Abū Qurra (d. early ninth century), student of John of Damascus, later Melkite Bishop of Ḥarrān and very likely the father of Arabic ecclesiastical literature (on Abū Qurra and his works see G. Graf, *Geschichte der Christlichen Arabischen Literatur*, Vol. II [4 vols. and index; Vatican City, 1944-53], pp. 7ff). Although Abū Qurra wrote in Greek as well as in Arabic and Syriac, Greek appears to have declined rapidly both as a written language and as a liturgical tongue among the Melkites. Despite Walzer's assertion that "educated native speakers of Greek can still be met in the Greek quarter of Baghdad in the second half of the 10th century," it is unlikely that the general use of Greek in the liturgy and writings (translations apart) of the Melkites survived the middle of the ninth century. See R. Walzer, "The Achievement of the Falasifa and their Eventual Failure," *Correspondance d'Orient, No. 5: Colloque sur la Sociologie Musulmane, Actes, 11-14 Septembre 1961*, Publications du Centre pour l'Etude des Problèmes du Monde Musulman Contemporain (Bruxelles, 1961?), p. 352; Graf, II, 5; Karalevskij, *DHGE*, III, col. 588.

[12] For an example drawn from the late sixteenth century see the short manual summarizing Melkite laws of inheritance, written by the Melkite Patriarch Mīkhā'īl al-Ḥamawī (1577-81) and found in manuscript in the Vatican (Biblioteca Apostolica Vaticana, *Vaticanus Arabicus*, Mīkhā'īl al Ḥamawī, Kitāb Farīḍah al-Mawārīth, MS 54). The many works of a later Melkite patriarch, Macarius

of the Prophet in its fullness, even as the Islamic civilization long since fully shaped, could perfectly be the possession only of Muslims. Not until the late seventeenth century did the weather begin to turn.

In the latter half of the sixteenth century, and as a sideward thrust of the Counter-Reformation, the papacy confided to the Society of Jesus "extraordinary missions" among the Eastern Churches. The immediate objective in Syria was to remind the faltering Maronites of their fealty to the Roman see and, that accomplished, to initiate a full-scale missionary assault against the non-Uniate Churches of the East, to wit: the Melkite, Nestorian, Jacobite, and Armenian.

Although the 1580's had witnessed some probing, no Jesuit mission made its appearance in Syria until the 1620's.[13] In the interim, however, the Latins had not been

---

al-Za'īm (1647-72), provide seventeenth-century cases in point; see for example Macarius' chronology of Melkite patriarchs (Biblioteca Apostolica Vaticana, *Vaticanus Arabicus*, Makāriyūs al-Za'īm, Asāmī Baṭārikah Anṭākiyah min Buṭrus al-Rasūl wa alladhīnā ma'ahu, MS 689 [hereafter cited as Makāriyūs al-Za'īm]). That the Uniate Melkite metropolitan of Sidon, Euthymius al-Ṣayfī (d. 1723), the extent of whose grasp of classical Arabic may be seen in his many letters to the Congregation of the Propaganda (see for example Arch. Prop., *SOCG*, Vol. 540, fol. 355, al-Ṣayfī to S. Congregation, 2/24/1701; *ibid.*, Vol. 598, fol. 195, al-Ṣayfī to S. Congregation, 5/26/1714), could have earned the sobriquet, *quffah al-'ilm* ("the basket of learning"), may perhaps stand as testimony to the indignities to which the Christians habitually subjected literary Arabic (Bibliothèque Orientale de Beyrouth, Mīkhā'īl Burayk, *Asāmī al-Baṭārikah fī Anṭākiyah min 'Ahd Buṭrus al-Rasūl ilā al-Ān*, MS 14, fol. 142 [hereafter cited as Burayk, *Asāmī*]).

[13] Concerning the mission of the Jesuit, Eliano, in 1580-82 see A. Rabbath (ed.), *Documents inédits pour servir à l'histoire du christianisme en orient*, Vol. 1 (2 vols.; Paris, 1905-21), pp. 195-

idle. In 1583 Vatican presses produced the first Arabic Bible (and remained the sole source of printed Bibles until the Protestants entered the competition in the nineteenth century). The creation of the Greek College in Rome in 1577, at the instance of Pope Gregory XIII, was followed, scarcely seven years later, by the establishment of the Maronite College.[14] And years before the Jesuits took up positions in Syria the Maronite College had graduated at least one noteworthy scholar, Gabriel Sionita (Jibrā'īl al-Ṣahyūnī, 1577-1648), pioneer Arabist, Syriac scholar, teacher in Rome and holder of the Chair of Semitic Languages at the Collège Royal in Paris. The seventeenth and eighteenth centuries saw the emergence of a number of distinguished Roman-trained Maronite scholars—notably Abraham Ecchellensis (Ibrāhīm al-Haqilānī, 1605-64) and the remarkable Assemanus (al-Sim'ānī) family. And while it is to some extent true that these men had more influence in Europe than among their own people, their mere existence testified to a quickened intellectual impulse among the Maronite clergy and, through a re-

207, 211-304; concerning that of the Maltese monseigneur, Leonard Abel, in 1583-84 see L. Abel, *Une mission religieuse en Orient au xvi^e^ siècle: Relation adressée à Sixte-Quint par l'évêque de Sidon*, trans. A. d'Avril (Paris, 1866). The Jesuits and Capuchins were dispatched to Aleppo in 1626, at the command of Urban VIII and with the enthusiastic support of Louis XIII. The Carmelites followed hard upon them, and before mid-century these three orders were more or less firmly established in Aleppo and elsewhere in Syria (see J. Hajjar, *Les chrétiens uniates du Proche-Orient* [Paris, 1962], pp. 218-20). The Franciscans, as "custodians of the Holy Land," had long before been in evidence in Syria and had maintained contact with the Maronites, at least intermittently, during the fourteenth and fifteenth centuries (see Salibi, p. 121).

14 Rabbath, I, iii.

newed curiosity about their community's history, an incipient interest in the Arabo-Islamic literary culture with which it had become associated.[15] Nor for that matter was this intellectual stirring confined to the more accomplished scholars who, for the most part, took up residence in Europe. After the first quarter of the seventeenth century Latin missions, Jesuit and other, as well as Maronites returned from study in Rome, could be found among the Maronites imparting to some of their protégés at least the rudiments of Catholic theology and often more than the rudiments of Latin, Italian, and French, thus helping to attach the mountaineers more firmly to Rome and providing an élite among them with the linguistic keys to European civilization.[16] At the hands of Maronites and

[15] On Sionita see Graf, III, 351-53; on Ecchellensis, *ibid.*, 354-59; on the Assemanus family, *ibid.*, 444-59 *et passim.*

[16] Largely, it would appear, on the basis of an oft-cited passage from Volney's late eighteenth-century travel account, modern scholars, Gibb and Salibi among them, perhaps tend to minimize the extent and quality of the Maronite education which was sponsored directly or indirectly by the Latin missions, not to mention the French factories (C. F. Volney, *Voyage en Égypte et en Syrie, 1783-5*, Vol. I [2 vols.; 2d ed.; Paris, 1825], pp. 387-88; H. A. R. Gibb and H. Bowen, *Islamic Society and the West*, Vol. I, Pt. ii [1 vol., 2 pts.; London, 1950, 1957], p. 249; Salibi, pp. 123-26). It is to be noted that, from the time of their establishment in Syria, the Latins—the Jesuits particularly—saw education of native Christian youths as a sure means of capturing them for the Unia. We know indeed that instruction was provided by the Jesuits in seventeenth-century Aleppo and Damascus, in a milieu far less hospitable than that of the Lebanon; we may surmise, too, that however limited in scope, however irregularly provided, the instruction thus imparted must have been in excess of any available through any other agency (on Latin attempts at education in seventeenth-century Aleppo and Damascus, see Rabbath, I, 380, Queyrot à l'ambassadeur, Alep, 6/29/1629; *ibid.*, I, 380-81, Queyrot

other Uniates, as well as Latins, works of theological, apologetical, and liturgical significance began the arduous passage from Latin and Syriac into Arabic. Even the *Summa* of the Angelic Doctor had made its way into the language of the Prophet by the early eighteenth century.[17]

The linguistic Arabization of the Melkite community of Syria showed a somewhat different pattern. Unlike the physically isolated mountaineer Maronites, who even today retain their Syriac liturgy, the Melkites seem to have adopted Arabic as their principal liturgical tongue before the seventeenth century.[18] Three factors explain the yielding of the Syriac and the much less utilized Greek liturgies before the Arabic: the virtual elimination of Syriac as a vernacular tongue; Melkite concentration in urban centers dominated by the Arabic literary culture of Sunnī Islam;[19] and the fast-fading influence of the Greek literary culture of specifically Byzantine Orthodoxy.

---

à un père S.J., Alep, 2/28/1631; *ibid.*, I, 402, Relation par Amieu, Alep, 1/16/1651; *ibid.*, II, 239, Relation par Poirresson en 1654 et 1655). And quite apart from the educational efforts of those Roman-trained Maronites who returned to their homeland, one must take seriously the special educational role of the French factories in seventeenth- and eighteenth-century Syria (*see below*, pp. 32ff).

[17] The first complete Arabic translation of the *Summa* was the work of Isḥāq ibn Jubayr (d. 1721), a Uniate won over from the Jacobites and ordained by the Maronite patriarch (Graf, IV, 47-50).

[18] J. Nasrallah, "Euthyme II Karmé (Karma)," *DHGE*, XVI, col. 54.

[19] This fact would also tend to support the assumption that the adoption of vernacular Arabic proceeded more quickly among the Melkites than among other Syrian Christians. For an analysis of the rise and decline of the episcopal sees of the Melkites would almost surely reveal that the urban character of that community

With reference to this last point, it is to be remembered that the Muslim advance across Anatolia, initiated in the eleventh century, ended only with the fall of Constantinople in 1453 and the destruction of the Empire of Constantine. Between 1453 and the Ottoman conquest of Syria in 1516, moreover, the Orthodox of Syria (still under Mamlūk rule) had been effectively cut off from the Patriarchate of Constantinople, which the Sunnī Ottomans—with an eye toward governing the Orthodox population of the Balkans—had reconstituted as an arm of their own administration and with ecclesiastical and civil powers broader than those enjoyed by the Great Church in the days of the Christian empire. By the time the Ottoman conquest of Syria brought the Orthodox there into renewed and intimate contact with the Greek Church, the Melkite Patriarchate of Antioch had undergone several centuries of comparatively independent ecclesiastical and, such as it was, cultural development. It must have been

---

became even more marked during the first century or so after the Ottoman conquest of Syria. Some of the data for such an analysis is to be found in Makāriyūs al-Zaʿīm, fols. 127-28; Burayk, *Asāmī*, fol. 135; Būlus al-Zaʿīm, *Nukhbah Safrah al-Baṭrīrk Makāriyūs al-Ḥalabī bi Qalam Waladihi al-Shammās Būlus*, ed. Q. al-Bāshā (Ḥarīṣā, Lebanon, 1912), pp. 19, 20, 25, 67 *et passim*; H. Zayat et N. Edelby, "Les sièges épiscopaux du patriarcat melkite d'Antioche en 1658 d'après un document inédit du Patriarche Macaire III Zaʿīm," *Proche-Orient Chrétien*, III (1953), 340-50; J. Nasrallah, "Chronologie des Patriarches d'Antioche de 1500 à 1634," *Proche-Orient Chrétien*, VI (1956), 294-311, VII (1957), 26-43, 207-17, 291-304; L. Shaykhū et C. Charon, "Usqufīyah al-Rūm al-Kātūlīk fī Bayrūt," *Al-Machriq*, VIII (1905), 193-204; C. Charon, "Silsilah Asāqifah al-Malikīyīn fī Qārā wa Yabrūd wa Tadmur wa Zaḥlah wa al-Zabadānī," *Al-Machriq*, XIII (1910), 328-37; C. Charon, "Silsilah Maṭārinah Kursī Ḥalab," *Al-Machriq*, XI (1908), 536-45; C. Charon, "Silsilah Maṭārinah Kursī Ṣūr," *Al-Machriq*, IX (1906), 412-16.

during this era that the Arabic liturgy made its most rapid advance; and its apparently total victory by the seventeenth century initiated, among Melkites even more than Maronites, an energetic attempt, in the relative security and increasing prosperity of the early Ottoman period, to render into Arabic a significant amount of Greek and Syriac ecclesiastical literature.[20] Melkite translations were not unaffected by the Vatican's printing of an Arabic Bible as well as those Arabic liturgical books, grammars, and dictionaries, necessitated by the papacy's plans for non-Uniate Syrian Christendom. That most of the translations wrought by Melkites, Maronites, and Latins were of not the slightest interest to Arab Muslim society and were, by the literary standards of even that intellectually moribund community, abominable is altogether beside the point. However modest, they marked the prelude to the second age of transmission.

## IV

CONCURRENTLY the Latins were responsible for much more than an accelerated program of translation. Assured in the course of the second half of the seventeenth century that the Uniate Maronites rested more firmly in the Roman bosom than at any time since the Crusades, the mis-

[20] The most prolific Melkite translators of the seventeenth century were Meletius al-Karmah, metropolitan of Aleppo (1612-34) and, as Euthymius, patriarch of Antioch (1634-35); and his protégé and successor as metropolitan of Aleppo, Meletius al-Za'īm (as Macarius, patriarch of Antioch, 1647-72). On the career and works of al-Karmah see Burayk, *Asāmī*, fol. 133; Makāriyūs al-Za'īm, fol. 130; Nasrallah, *DHGE*, XVI, cols. 53-57; Graf, III, 91-94; concerning the works of al-Za'īm see Burayk, *Asāmī*, fols. 137-38; Graf, III, 94-110.

sionaries could devote their energies to the healing, after their fashion, of the Great and lesser "schisms" represented by the Melkites and the Jacobites, Nestorians and Armenians. They pursued their task with certain advantages. Their discipline and learning were, by contemporary Eastern standards, impressive; and nowhere is the missionary's awareness of his own intellectual superiority more apparent than in a Jesuit's easy dismissal of the Melkite Patriarch Macarius al-Zaʿīm (surely one of the most learned Eastern hierarchs of the seventeenth century) as merely a good preacher who knows nothing of theology or philosophy.[21] The Jesuit, inadvertently, was describing the gap separating Europe from a world where commentary, compilation, and rhetoric had become the measures of intellectual excellence.

The attitude of the Syrian Christians toward the Western clerics was, moreover, not unfriendly; the judgment of the Orthodox of Syria, for one, derived less from memory of the Latin sack of Constantinople, 400 years before, than from a millennium of Muslim domination. There is also some evidence that between the exit of the Crusaders and the arrival of the missionaries the Christians of Syria had arrived at something of a nondoctrinally based *modus vivendi*. On all sides the death of theological speculation and the meager learning of the clergy had reduced many questions of doctrine to near irrelevance. We know that the early 1540's had witnessed an attempt at union between the Maronite and Melkite Churches—an attempt which it would seem was frustrated less by doctrinal divergence than by the opposition of the Great Church and perhaps by Ottoman uneasiness over an arrangement

[21] Rabbath, I, 402, Relation par Amieu, Alep, 1/16/1651.

which threatened to bring within a single fold the semi-autonomous mountaineers and the most numerous Christian element of urban Syria.[22] We know too that the Melkite Church could, in the 1580's, spawn a patriarch who had never heard of the Council of Florence,[23] and that as late as 1650 the Uniate Maronites were led by a prelate who promised excommunication to any of his flock who made his confession before a Latin priest.[24]

At the same time, and perhaps as a by-product of the losses and dislocations of the Mamlūk period, the sense of "difference" among the generality of Syrian Christians had yielded in some measure to an awareness of the advantages of cooperation in face of the unitary Muslim temporal power to which they were in common subjection. In 1659 a Melkite patriarch, returned from seven years in "the lands of the Christians," was greeted on the edge of Aleppo by Christians of all sects,[25] prelates of one communion were known to use their good offices to settle disputes arising within another,[26] and at least on the Great Feasts and other special occasions the laity and clergy of one sect were known to frequent the Churches of others.[27]

Throughout most of the seventeenth century, then, there is little indication that the Latins were regarded by the Melkites as a threat. Their schools were, on the whole, welcomed; their visits to the clergy and laity well received; and the material aid they rendered in times of

[22] Makāriyūs al-Zaʿīm, fol. 127.

[23] Karalevskij, *DHGE*, III, col. 639.

[24] Rabbath, I, 396-97, Relation par Amieu, Alep, 1/16/1651.

[25] Būlus al-Zaʿīm, pp. 73, 75, 76, 78-80.

[26] Burayk, *Asāmī*, fols. 121-22.

[27] Būlus al-Zaʿīm, p. 80 & n.

famine and plague gratefully acknowledged.[28] The hierarchy was further soothed by the willingness of the Sacred Congregation to subsidize to some extent the more cooperative among them and by the promise of supplementary succor from the Very Catholic French King[29]—for religious and more mundane reasons protector of the Latin missionaries and aspiring protector of the Christian subjects of the Sultan.

In the early eighteenth century, moreover, the government of the Melkite patriarchate of Antioch lay in ruins. Ottoman rule, even in its heyday, had not been an unmixed blessing. In the last analysis the conquest of Sultan Selīm—despite the considerable degree of peace and stability introduced into Syria—was for the Melkites but the latest phase of the *essentially* hostile Muslim domination

[28] Rabbath, I, 380, Queyrot à l'ambassadeur, Alep, 6/29/1629; *ibid.*, I, 380-81, Queyrot à un père S.J., Alep, 2/28/1631; *ibid.*, I, 402, Relation par Amieu, Alep, 1/16/1651; *ibid.*, I, 53, Relation par Poirresson, Seyde, 4/16/1653; *ibid.*, I, 451-52, 458-59, Relation de la mission d'Alep en 1662; *ibid.*, II, 240, 244, Relation par Poirresson en 1654 et 1655; *ibid.*, II, 207, 220, Relation par Poirresson en 1653; Joseph Besson, *La Syrie et la terre sainte au XVII^e^ siècle* (Paris, 1862), pp. 21, 68, 71-72; *Lettres édifiantes et curieuses écrites des missions étrangères*, Vol. I (5 vols.; Toulouse, 1810), pp. 96-99, 132, Nacchi à Tamburini, 1718 or 1719.

[29] The Melkite patriarch Ignatius solicited, and may have received, the subsidies of the Propaganda in the early 1630's (see Karalevskij, *DHGE*, III, col. 641). On the more or less regular subsidies received from the Propaganda by Euthymius al-Ṣayfī, Melkite metropolitan of Sidon (1683-1723), see Arch. Prop., *CP*, Vol. 75, fol. 262, Euthymius to Innocent III, 5/20/1722, in Arabic. The coupling of Roman subsidies with French diplomatic pressures is well illustrated by the case of Ignatius Peter, Uniate contender for the "Jacobite" patriarchal dignity (see Arch. Prop., *SOCG*, Vol. 530, fols. 28-29, de Chateauneuf à Altiery, Adrianople, 11/20/1697, in French).

which over a period of 900 years had helped reduce the ancient Church to that sorry status which is perhaps the destiny of the socially and politically disabled minority. Quite apart from this central fact of Antiochian Melkite history, however, the advent of Selīm meant that the ecclesiastical independence (within, of course, the definitions of Muslim sacred law) enjoyed by the Syrians for several centuries before was to yield gradually to a reassertion of the influence and then the direct authority of the Greek Patriarchate of Constantinople.

From the inception of Ottoman rule in Syria the ecumenical patriarch was established as the sole channel of communication between the Antiochian patriarchate and the Ottoman central government and, subject only to the latter's discretion, the final arbiter in its civil and ecclesiastical affairs. Had the enormous power wielded by the ecumenical see as a department of the Ottoman central administration been intelligently and decently employed in the sixteenth and seventeenth centuries, the effect on the Melkites of Syria might have been salutary. But, for reasons which cannot detain us here, the Great Church in this period was not characterized by a particularly high degree of either integrity or stability. And until Greek prelates designated by the Patriarchate of Constantinople assumed, in the course of the eighteenth century, direct control over the Syrian see, the Greek Church played something resembling the role of well-paid but dishonest broker between contending factions at Antioch.[30]

[30] The fact that Melkite patriarchal candidates could receive their *berets* of investiture only through the agency of the ecumenical patriarchate provided the basis of Greek power to decide between Syrian contenders. During the two centuries before Constantinople's assumption of direct control there was scarcely a

It must be pointed out at once, however, that had Constantinople's interventions been models of wisdom and probity there was really little assurance that Ottoman officials in Syria could or would have implemented them. The Ottoman conquest had by no means destroyed (nor was it its intention to destroy) all pockets of local authority in the Arab provinces, and these from the outset mediated relations between the Sultan and his Arabic-speaking subjects. In Syria the most obvious and important survivals of local authority were to be seen in the mountain refuge of the Lebanon where, less than seventy years after Selīm took Syria, a heterodox Muslim (and therefore by Sunnī Muslim definition not wholly legitimate) *amīr* could be found protecting, with perfect impunity, a Melkite patriarch fleeing the wrath of the Ottoman governor of Damascus,[31] and where, some forty years later, the redoubtable (and even more heterodox) Fakhr al-Dīn successfully maintained in power a patriarch whose deposition by the ecumenical see had been solemnly confirmed by an imperial edict.[32] It is important to note, in connection with the formation of a Uniate offshoot of the Melkite Church, that the Lebanese *amīrs* were the natural allies of those who, like themselves, stood on the questionable side of Ottoman legality.

patriarchal reign free of ill-advised Greek interference. Cyril al-Za'īm (1672-1720), for example, was deposed (and invested) no less than three times (see Burayk, *Asāmī*, fols. 139-41).

[31] Patriarch Joachim was obliged to flee Damascus in 1583 because of his inability to pay either the debts hanging over his see or the sums demanded by the *wālī* of Damascus for exertions in his behalf. Joachim took refuge in the Biqā', under the protection of the Shi'ite house of Ḥarfūsh (Būlus al-Za'īm, p. 28n).

[32] The patriarch was Ignatius 'Aṭīyah, 1619-34 (see Burayk, *Asāmī*, fols. 119-24).

But even before the *amīrs* cast themselves clearly in the role of patrons of the Uniate communities, their semiautonomy had posed special problems for the Orthodox of Syria. Because the Melkite hierarchy were regarded by Muslim law (and on one level regarded themselves) as officials of the temporal authority, the unity of the temporal authority was virtually a precondition for the unity of the patriarchate. With the widest geographic distribution of any sect in Syria, whether Christian *or* Muslim,[33] any pronounced political fragmentation was quickly reflected in the related ecclesiastical institution. Obviously the Maronites—located for the most part in the clearly circumscribed and relatively isolated area of the Lebanon and under the semiautonomous political authority of their own or heterodox Muslim *amīrs*—were not confronted with the same problem. As we shall see, their geographic situation, together with the fact of their allegiance to Rome, explains most of the differences in attitude between them and the Orthodox Melkites toward the several nationalist movements which were to emerge in Syria in the nineteenth and twentieth centuries.

The Lebanese *amīrs* were not the only local forces which could, consciously and otherwise, assist Latin penetration by standing between the Ottoman-supported Patriarchate of Constantinople and the Orthodox of Syria. The power of the central government, often shadowy in the mountain and in certain rural areas, was less than complete even in the Sunnī-dominated urban centers with

[33] Given our knowledge of the demography of Syria in the seventeenth century, this statement is obviously impossible to confirm statistically. It tends to be strongly confirmed, however, by analysis of the diocesan distribution of the Melkites in this era (see *above*, pp. 20-21, n. 19).

their significant Melkite minorities. The chief officials of the Ottoman provincial administration—the *Wālīs* and *Qāḍīs*—were merely presiding officers over the numerous self-contained groups which comprised Ottoman urban society. They were, moreover, rotated on an almost annual basis, a circumstance that not only tended to affect adversely the integrity of their government (and glimpses of this could be seen even in the sixteenth century) but inevitably shifted much of the responsibility for administrative continuity and order (or disorder) to local elements. The diffuse nature of authority characteristic of large cities such as Aleppo and Damascus, where perhaps the majority of the Melkites were concentrated, served to frustrate on more than one occasion the government of the ecumenical patriarchate as it related to the Orthodox of Syria.[34]

## V

WITHAL, the creation of a sizable Uniate body from the Melkite and other Churches of Syria would have been improbable had it not been for that radical shift in the power relationship between the Ottoman Empire and

[34] Patriarch Michael V, deposed by the Damascenes in 1581 and twice reinvested by Constantinople, was able neither to eliminate an opponent who enjoyed Damascene support nor to reestablish himself in the patriarchal residence in Damascus (Makāriyūs al-Za'īm, fol. 128; Burayk, *Asāmī*, fols. 110-12; Būlus al-Za'īm, p. 28n). Patriarch Cyril IV, despite the support of the ecumenical patriarchate, was, in 1624-25, unable to take up residence in Damascus or to discipline an insubordinate metropolitan of Aleppo (Burayk, *Asāmī*, fols. 118-24). Analogous examples drawn from the sixteenth, seventeenth, and eighteenth centuries are abundantly available.

Europe which took place over the period from roughly 1650 to 1750. For it was not until the objects of Latin proselytizing were reasonably convinced that entry into the Unia would, through the European and certain local Syrian connections obtained thereby, provide them with a range of possibility which adhesion to their ancestral faith could not that large numbers of them declared openly for Rome. By 1700 such was the case; and for the first time the Syrian Christian in search of an added measure of security and material advantage possessed an alternative to conversion to Islam.

The institutions of the great Ottoman age could, by the turn of the seventeenth century, be counted among the dead and dying—a fact which the Treaties of Karlowitz (1699) and Passarowitz (1718) eloquently confirmed. French influence in Ottoman affairs was strong and growing stronger, a circumstance which reflected not only the changing balance of power between the Ottoman Empire and Europe but the cordial relations which common hostility to the House of Hapsburg had bred between the infidel Sultan and the Eldest Daughter of the Church.[35]

[35] As late as 1670 the French consul at Sidon could write that "there is no nation, in the states of the Grand Seigneur, less regarded than the French." By contrast, a successor in 1685 could dwell upon the honors shown the ambassadors of "the greatest King on earth," and in 1694 could bask in the special regard with which the *wālīs* favored the French nation (A. E., B[1]1017, fol. 9, Bonnecorse au [Ministre], Seyde, 2/1/1670; *ibid.*, fol. 31, l'Empereur au [Ministre], Seyde, 1/22/1685; *ibid.*, fol. 66, l'Empereur au [Ministre], Seyde, 7/15/1694). Even the English ambassador in 1692, Thomas Coke, took time to comment upon "the French Ambassador's familiarity with the cheife Ministers . . . and with severall of the Visir's family" (S. P. 97/20, fol. 237, Coke to Earl of Notingham, Istanbul, Feb. 18/28, 1692.

And even before the Capitulations of 1740 undid most of the Ottoman legal opposition to Latin proselytizing among the Sultan's Christian subjects,[36] French diplomatic protection had more or less successfully cancelled out the opposition of the non-Uniate Churches.

The fact that not until 1839 were the Uniate Churches (the traditionally Uniate Maronites excepted) accorded legal recognition by the Ottoman government must not be overemphasized. Its own laws notwithstanding, the Ottoman government, throughout the crucial seventeenth century, was largely indifferent to the missionary assault: an indifference which stemmed in part from Ottoman interest in maintaining friendly relations with France; in part from the absence of consistent pressure from the Patriarchate of Constantinople; and in part from the contemptuous tolerance with which the Sultan customarily viewed the internal struggles of his Christian subjects so long as they met their largely financial obligations toward the government. A French observer in Aleppo in 1683 could comment that the Turks were unconcerned about the "return" of the "schismatics" to Rome since the missionaries were careful to remind the neophytes to render unto Caesar, etc.[37] The quite stationary Ottoman Muslim mentality could not free itself of the belief that somehow "infidelity constitutes a single *millet*."[38] Ottoman official-

[36] The crucial articles are 82 and 84 of the Capitulations of 1740, for the French text of which see Gabriel Noradounghian, *Recueil d'actes internationaux de l'empire ottoman*, Vol. I (3 vols.; Paris, 1897-1902), pp. 299-300.

[37] Laurent d'Arvieux, *Mémoires du Chevalier d'Arvieux*, Vol. VI (6 vols.; Paris, 1735), p. 420.

[38] From a *fatwā* issued in Aleppo in 1762 by the Ḥanafī, Sulaymān al-Manṣūrī, following an outbreak between the Orthodox and

dom, parochial and still supremely confident of the Empire's strength, had little real awareness of the threat to traditional Ottoman society implicit in the creation of the Unia. They failed utterly to comprehend that the Latin advance represented an early and enormously important aspect of Western penetration and that its success was a partial index to the extent of the breakdown of Ottoman polity and an early example of the regrouping of Near Eastern society around European and certain indigenous sources of authority, notably the heterodox Lebanese princes.

Nor was the effectiveness of the missionary unrelated to economic considerations. For as the seventeenth century drew to a close, the Melkite men of commerce—the lay leadership, a few of them mission-educated—whether as clients of European merchants or moving toward a more independent position, had grown acutely aware of the advantages of consular protection and no less aware of the intimate connection between consular protection and membership in the Unia. The foreign protection which was of greatest consequence to Syrian Christian men of commerce in the late seventeenth and early eighteenth century was neither conferred through scarcely attainable Royal or ambassadorial patents, nor through naturalization, nor yet through appointment to the office of dragoman.[39] As to the notorious and somewhat more

---

Uniate Melkites; quoted in Ḥaydar al-Shihābī, *Al-Ghurar al-Ḥisān fī Akhbār Abnā' al-Zamān*, ed. A. Rustum, F. A. Bustānī (Beirut, 1933), p. 58.

[39] A patent of protection granted an Aleppine Maronite by Ambassador Desalleurs in 1714, and a Royal patent issued to another Aleppine Maronite at the instance of the Propaganda in 1729, both met with strong objections from the French consuls at Aleppo, one of whom argued that such practice was contrary to the Capitula-

accessible *beret* of honorary dragoman it is to be observed that while this patent of protection was of incalculable importance in the consolidation, preservation, and later prosperity of the Uniate Melkites, it was hardly crucial to their early development. Before the 1720's the Syrian

---

tions and that, moreover, the consuls encountered enough difficulty protecting those in possession of *berets* (patents) confirmed by the Porte (A. E., $B^1$81, fols. 73-75, Peleran [fils] à de Maurepas, Alep, 7/11/1729; *ibid.*, fol. 76, Desalleurs à Peleran [père], Istanbul, 6/1/1714). We hear of yet another Maronite, "Jean Nader" (Ḥannā Nādir), who managed to obtain a Royal patent of protection some years before his appointment in 1725 as dragoman of the French vice-consulate at Acre (A. E., $B^1$1020, fol. 213, Poullard au Conseil de Marine, Seyde, 10/1/1717). Two requests for naturalization, made in 1708 and 1720 by the Maronite dragoman of the French vice-consulate in Tripoli, were both denied on grounds that naturalization was usually granted only on condition that the naturalized reside in France and leave that country only with the King's consent (A. E., $B^1$1114, unnumbered fol. between fols. 235 and 236, de Boismont à de Pontchartrain, Tripoli, 8/20/1708; A. E., $B^1$1115, fol. 190 [Demaillet's opinion concerning the request made by Torbey in 1720]). Poullard, consul at Sidon, complained in 1717 of native merchants who, having obtained the King's letters of naturalization on condition that they remain in France, returned to the Levant and not only competed commercially with the French but had to be defended by the French against the Ottoman authorities. The only example cited by Poullard, however, was a native Aleppine born of Venetian-Polish parents (A. E., $B^1$1020, fols. 209-13, Poullard au Conseil de Marine, Seyde, 10/1/1717). The English, for whom the religious motivation was scarcely operative, conferred Royal or ambassadorial patents of protection, not to mention naturalization, even more rarely than did the French. As for the office of dragoman (as opposed to honorary dragoman), a thorough examination of the extant papers of the French consulate at Aleppo during the seventeenth and eighteenth centuries fails to reveal a single Syrian Christian appointee. The French factory at Sidon, on the other hand, relied upon Maronites as second dragomans throughout much of the eighteenth century (see *below*, p. 40, n. 52). Native Christians, mainly Maronites, also served as dragomans to the French vice-consulates at Acre and Tripoli (*ibid.*).

Christians holding *berets* as honorary dragomans were relatively few[40] and it was only in the latter half of the century that traffic in these patents assumed the flood proportions which were to make them synonyms for fraud. It is rather in those circumstances out of which the *beret* of honorary dragoman evolved that one glimpses the types of foreign protection most pertinent to the beginnings of the Melkite schism.

The native Christian who served the early European merchants in Syria was at the outset little more than a servant-interpreter. It is evident, however, that as the seventeenth century wore onward the Syrian Christian began to join to the function of interpreter that of agent, receiving from the European merchant or merchants employing him a percentage on the buying and selling in which he participated.[41] Expanding trade on his own account, the while retaining his affiliation with the Europeans, represented merely a logical step beyond. Only rarely, and then of course surreptitiously, did the increasingly independent native merchant enjoy even an approximation of the lower customs duties which the Capitulations accorded the Europeans.[42] On the other hand satis-

[40] An assertion based upon close examination of the extant papers of the French establishments in Syria during the seventeenth and eighteenth centuries.

[41] A. E., $B^1$1036, unnumbered fol., "Mémoire sur les dragomans arabes . . . ," Seyde, November 1773.

[42] By virtue of the Capitulations of 1673 the French paid duties of 3 percent on imports and exports, rather than the 5 percent paid by the Sultan's subjects (see New Article 5 of the Capitulations of 1673, in Noradounghian, I, 144). Other European nations were not long in acquiring the same advantage; the English, for example, were accorded it through Article 53 of their Capitulations of 1675 (*ibid.*, I, 162). At least the French merchants, however, en-

fied, we may assume, with a smaller margin of profit than was his European patron, fully conversant with the latter's business affairs and better equipped by virtue of birth and tongue to exploit local commercial opportunities, the Syrian Christian soon found himself in a competitive position *vis-à-vis* the European merchant and favored with a singular advantage over the Muslim. That the erstwhile servant-interpreter was emerging as a serious economic rival must have been clear to the Europeans by the beginning of the eighteenth century. That little was done to inhibit his further development only reflected the extent to which the often transient foreigner, confronted by the dual barrier of Arabic and Turkish and little acquainted with local usage, had grown dependent upon the services of his native protégés.[43] Let it be noted

---

gaged in the practice of shipping, under their own names and for a commission of 1 percent, goods belonging to other Europeans and to Syrian Christians. These latter thereby paid duties of 4 percent rather than 5 percent. For instance a contract dated Livorno, May 6, 1713, involved a French merchant at Aleppo who had shipped from Livorno, under his company's name, goods belonging to a Uniate Melkite of Aleppo (A. E., $B^1$77, fol. 435). Note also the complaint of a French consul at Aleppo concerning "the avidity of several Frenchmen who, in order to profit from a miserable commission, lend their names to strangers, be they English or subjects of the Sultan, to send merchandise to Marseille, [and] do considerable wrong to the trade of the Nation" (A. E., $B^1$78, fols. 118-19, Mémoire de Peleran, Alep, 11/25/1716).

[43] *Ibid.* Consider too the assertion of the French consul at Sidon in 1767 that however desirable the current regulations forbidding French merchants to buy and sell through their native agents, such regulations were impossible to enforce (A. E., $B^1$1033, unnumbered fol., de Clairambault à Monseigneur, Seyde, 1/29/1767). Soon the consuls were no longer even alluding to any such regulations, the balance between European and Syrian merchants having shifted to the latter's favor. The advantage was not to be recovered by the

too that the French consuls' dragomans, themselves almost invariably Frenchmen, who were intended initially to perform the interpreter's function for the factory as well as the consul, were often disqualified for serving the former by indifferent linguistic skill, the press of strictly consular duties, and an imperfect knowledge of commerce.[44]

Now throughout his progress from servant-interpreter to autonomous merchant the Syrian Christian enjoyed some form of European protection, though until and, to some extent, even after the emergence of the *beret* of honorary dragoman as the protective shield *par excellence* this protection was of a largely informal nature. Consisting originally in consular intervention on behalf of a protégé threatened by Ottoman legal (or illegal) action for reasons usually arising from the factory's relations with the Ottoman authorities,[45] as time went on it was extended to *dhimmī* tax disputes with provincial officials[46] and of

---

Europeans until the post-Napoleonic era when the English particularly were once more propelled eastward, this time as a consequence of rapid industrialization at home.

[44] See A. E., B¹1116, fol. 49, le Maire à [de Maurepas], Tripoli, 2/15/1726.

[45] As in Sidon in 1698 when all the native Christians in the service of the French factory were imprisoned briefly and subjected to the bastinade for no reason other than the *wālī's* quarrel with the factory (A. E., B¹1017, fols. 150-51, l'Empereur à [de Pontchartrain], Seyde, 7/?/1698).

[46] In 1708, for example, Ibrāhīm Pasha of Sidon demanded from the population the annual tax on houses and gardens, oblivious to the fact that it had been collected scarcely a month before by his predecessor as *wālī*. The consul's intervention was inspired by the flight of virtually the entire Christian population (including those individuals in the service of the French) to the Mountain. All commerce thus came to a standstill. The consul prevailed upon the *wālī* to settle for one-half the sum of the annual tax. Since the Jews could do no better than settle for two-thirds, and the unhappy

course to the problems inspired by Latin proselytizing. Such intervention found no sanction in Ottoman law[47] and its success or lack of it depended on the *de facto* influence enjoyed by the consuls and factories on the local scene, whether as a reflection of the ambassador's influence at the Porte or growing out of peculiarly local circumstances. Let us once more remind ourselves that beginning with the last decades of the seventeenth century the European's influence increased steadily; and his word, more often than not, was treated with some deference not only by the Ottoman authorities[48] but also, in Sidon and elsewhere along the coast, by the Shihābī and Druze *amīrs* who were in the process of fastening their grip over the

---

Muslims were obliged to pay the full amount, the Christians emerged as distinctly the favored element (A. E., B¹1018, pp. 377-80, Mémoire d'Estelle, Seyde, 1/20/1708). Note also the joint intervention by the English and French consuls at Aleppo in 1713 to exempt their honorary dragomans and other protégés from payment of the poll tax (properly *jizyah* though usually termed *kharāj* in the contemporary documents); see A. E., B¹77, fols. 375-78, Peleran à de Pontchartrain, Alep, 11/24/1713.

[47] New Article 1 of the Capitulations of 1673, which recognized a French protectorate over Latin clergy who were subjects of France—a protectorate which the French ambassadors strove to interpret loosely enough to include non-Latin Uniates—must be regarded as the slightest of legal justifications (for the relevant text see Noradounghian, I, 143). Not more substantial was Article 14 (*ibid.*, I, 139) which exempted dragomans, "soient francs," from payment of the *jizyah* and all other taxes.

[48] See *above*, p. 36, n. 46. The consuls' intervention concerning payment of the poll tax by Aleppine Christian protégés in 1713, for example, was, by the French consul's admission, based on nothing more than "the voluntary agreements reached between us and the previous collectors of the *kharāj*, which, very far from being authorized by the Prince [Sultan], are peculations by those charged with the collection of this tax" (A. E., B¹77, fol. 376, Peleran à de Pontchartrain, Alep, 11/24/1713).

Lebanon.[49] Even consuls of uncertain prestige, however, developed the habit of intervention since an assault against a native protégé, guilty or innocent, represented an assault against the factory with which he was associated. The Syrian Christian had become too integral a part of the factory's life, too useful, too much acquainted with its affairs, its secrets, strengths, and weaknesses to be abandoned to his *dhimmī* devices in time of trouble.[50]

Such solicitude, however, was as characteristic of the Protestant English as the Catholic French and in itself hardly sustains a thesis connecting the emergence of the Uniate Melkites to the phenomenon of consular protection and to the enhanced economic opportunity acquired therefrom. On the other hand, several significant details distinguished the French from the English relationship to their protégés. There were, to begin with, more and larger French factories in Syria (at Sidon, indeed, a city crucial to the genesis of the Uniate Melkites, the French factory

[49] The death in 1707 of the Shihābī *amīr*, Bashīr I, was proclaimed by the French consul at Sidon "a great loss . . . for he had always much esteemed [our nation] and on all occasions rendered it his services with amity . . ." (A. E., $B^1$1018, pp. 447-48, Estelle à de Pontchartrain, Seyde, 8/5/1707). On French relations with his successors and with certain Druze *amīrs*, see A. E., $B^1$1022, fol. 296, Emir Haïdar [*sic*] à le Maire, 6/?/1730?; A. E., $B^1$1023, fol. 124, Grimaud à Monseigneur, Seyde, 3/16/1732; *ibid.*, fol. 126, Emir Melhem [*sic*] à Grimaud, 2/?/1732; A. E., $B^1$1024, fol. 297, Arasy à Monseigneur, Seyde, 10/31/1739; A. E., $B^1$1026, unnumbered fol., Arasy à Monseigneur, Seyde, 1/30/1742. Finally let us note the remark of the consul at Sidon in 1745 that the King's protection is more respected by the Druze *amīrs* "than all the commandments of the Grand Seigneur" (*ibid.*, unnumbered fol., de Lane à Monseigneur, Seyde, 3/7/1745).

[50] See A. E., $B^1$1019, p. 87, Poullard à de Pontchartrain, Seyde, 3/18/1712.

was the only one in existence) and this obviously necessitated a greater number of protégés. Then too the France of that era was the France of Louis XIV and, by virtue of her ascendancy in Western Europe and her usefulness as the Sultan's sometime ally against the Hapsburgs, her ambassadors and consuls in the Ottoman Empire enjoyed an influence which, while not to be confused with power, was in excess of anything the English or any other Europeans could claim. The English, moreover, were little concerned with winning over the Syrian Christians to the Reformed Faith and only fitfully and half-heartedly preoccupied with confirming them in their ancestral denominations. By contrast the French left the Syrian Christians with little doubt that to enter and to endure in the factory's service was virtually the function of receptivity to the papal message. The unity of interest between the French establishments and "our missionaries"[51] was rarely called into question; the consuls and merchants, no less than the Latin and indigenous Uniate clergy, did their best to ensure that those received into the factory's service, and once received best protected, were those already, or in the process of becoming Uniate.[52] But this emphasis on

[51] Thus their usual designation in the French consular documentation.

[52] This is most clearly illustrated by, though hardly restricted to, the dragomans employed by the consular service proper. An Orthodox Melkite (or, as the French source would have it, a "schismatic Greek") appointed to the post of dragoman to the vice-consulate at Tripoli in 1697 was summarily dismissed a few months later "because of the aversion he has naturally for the French"; and not unnaturally his successor was a Maronite—"Chrestien Catholique ap.$^{le}$ et Romain . . . un fort honneste garçon . . ." (A. E., $B^1$1114, fol. 14, "Extrait d'une lettre des . . . marchands françois de Tripoly . . . ," 12/19/1697; *ibid.*, fol.

Catholicism as the precondition for protection was by no means restricted exclusively to those in or aspiring toward service to the French.

As French influence after 1680 achieved a new pervasiveness, the Syrian Christian trader could be seen edging toward a more independent, or at least more diversified, position in the commerce of Syria, notably the coastal trade between that province and Egypt. By the beginning of the eighteenth century Melkite traders in Sidon and elsewhere along the coast, as well as in the inland entrepôts of Aleppo and Damascus, had come to control a substantial segment of the traffic between Syria and Egypt. The Melkites of Sidon also appear to have comprised most of the owners, or operators under French ownership, of the smaller vessels plying the route between the Syrian ports, notably Sidon, and the Egyptian port of Damietta.[53]

---

13 [affidavit in favor of the Maronite, dated 12/18/1697 and signed by a number of missionaries stationed in Tripoli]). Despite the probability that the numerically and commercially preponderant Christian element in Sidon was Melkite, they were Maronites—Uniates long since—who occupied the post of second dragoman throughout most of the first half of the eighteenth century (A. E., $B^1$1021, fol. 303, de Cresmery au Conseil de Marine, Seyde, 9/12/1722; A. E., $B^1$1024, fol. 285, Arasy au Ministre, Seyde, 9/3/1739; A. E., $B^1$1036, unnumbered fols., Mémoire sur les dragomans arabes, Seyde, 11/?/1773). At Acre an Orthodox Melkite who, under consular and missionary pressures, appears to have made the transit to the Unia, served the vice-consulate from roughly 1675 to 1725, at which date the post passed under Maronite auspices and there remained into the 1770's (A. E., $B^1$1018, pp. 1015-16, Poullard à [Desalleurs], Seyde, 11/1/1711; A. E., $B^1$1036, unnumbered fols., Mémoire sur les dragomans arabes, Seyde, 11/?/1773; A. E., $B^1$1019, p. 116, Poullard à de Pontchartrain, Seyde, 5/3/1712; *ibid.*, pp. 127-28, Poullard à l'ambassadeur, Seyde, 4/27/1712).

[53] The Uniate Melkite metropolitan of Sidon, Euthymius al-

Concurrently, however, European corsairs were establishing themselves as the scourge of this coastal shipping and, in an altogether backhand manner, as missionaries of considerable effectiveness. Unleashed for the most part from Malta, these latter-day Crusaders, though devoted ostensibly to undoing exclusively infidel shipping, in practice tended to plunder any vessel ungraced by the pavilion of a Catholic prince. Now insofar as any in Syria could influence the corsairs they were the representatives of the Very Christian King, and inevitably the Syrian Christian whose property was exposed to the depredations of the corsairs, or who sought restitution of property already plundered by them, made his way to the French consuls.

Ṣayfī, alludes to the many Catholics of Sidon involved in the coastal trade (Arch. Prop., *SOCG*, vol. 540, fol. 355, Euthymius to Pope Clement, Sidon, 2/24/1701, in Arabic). A document of 1702 tells of a vessel coming to Acre from Damietta, commanded by a Melkite and carrying a cargo belonging mainly to Maronite and Melkite merchants (A. E., B¹1017, fol. 280, "Extrait de la chancellerie de Seyde . . . ," 6/6/1702). We hear in 1704 of a vessel belonging to and commanded by a Melkite, presumably of Sidon, and carrying cargo belonging to Syrian Christian merchants (*ibid.*, fols. 469-70, Mémoire d'Estelle, Seyde, 10/29/1704). The French vice-consul at Tripoli in 1711 mentions a vessel commanded by a Melkite of Tripoli but belonging to French merchants of that city (A. E., B¹1114, de Boismont à de Pontchartrain, Tripoli, 12/19/1711). Another document of 1711 cites the vessel of one "Mikhail" of Sidon, carrying English cargo and plying the coastal route to Alexandretta (*ibid.*, fol. 401, "Traduction de la lettre du Pacha de Tripoly . . . ," [late 1711]). French consular documentation from the first decade of the eighteenth century provides many similar examples. And we have the French ambassador's categorical remark, albeit in 1732, that most of the vessels plying the Syrian coast and calling at Damietta, Rosetta, and Alexandria belonged to Syrians (A. E., B¹405, unnumbered fols., de Villeneuve à Monsieur, Istanbul, 2/15/1732). The ambassador meant, of course, Syrian Christians.

The consuls, in effect, then referred him to the missionaries, for the tacit price of French intervention in these matters was unquestionably submission to Rome. By 1702 the consuls, with the blessings of Versailles, were issuing to Uniates certificates which noted the fact of their Catholicism and the nature of the merchandise charged to their accounts.[54] But let Poullard, French consul at Sidon in 1720, provide the most unambiguous description of this practice:

> When the Catholic Christians of this country need certificates for the security of their persons and their effects, I provide them gratis, after taking their oath

[54] "I have made known to the Greek archbishop of Sidon [the Uniate Melkite, Euthymius al-Ṣayfī] . . . His Majesty's good intentions towards him in favoring the Christians of the country and protecting them from the piracies these poor people suffer at the hands of the Maltese and Livornese corsairs." The consul at Sidon goes on to say that he is now issuing to Christians of that city certificates stating their religion and the merchandise charged to their accounts, taking care that the corsairs are not deprived of their just rewards (i.e., non-Catholic property); see A. E., $B^1$1017, fol. 256, l'Empereur à [de Pontchartrain], Seyde, 3/23/1702. There can be no doubt that in l'Empereur's parlance "Christian" is synonymous to "Uniate," for the King's dispensation almost certainly came at Rome's behest. The papacy had been moved to action by pleas such as that made by Euthymius al-Ṣayfī in a letter to Pope Clement, written early in 1701. Asserting with some exaggeration that all the Christian clergy and laity of Sidon were now Uniate, the prelate added: "In order that we may increase their steadfastness in obedience to the Holy Church we desire that there be lifted from them the injuries and oppression of the corsairs who at sea damage their livelihood and sustenance." Euthymius then asked Clement to instruct the "Sultan of France" to send "an unequivocal order . . . that the hand of the corsairs of the sea be lifted from the [Uniate] inhabitants of Sidon" (Arch. Prop., *SOCG*, Vol. 540, fol. 355, Euthymius to Pope Clement, Sidon, 2/24/1701, in Arabic).

and establishing that they have not lent their names to Turks and heretical Christians. I also give gratis to [native] commanders of vessels belonging to our nationals certificates in good form to prove to all corsairs that the ownership of these vessels and their cargoes are truly charged to the account of the French.[55]

While it would be idle to maintain that these certificates invariably dissuaded the corsairs they did represent protection of considerable efficacy and, in the event they failed, appeal to Rome for restitution or compensation was always possible and, at least in the long run, often successful. In 1718 Peleran, French consul at Aleppo, wrote informing the Propaganda that the Melkite Patriarch Athanasius al-Dabbās (who decades before had made his submission to Rome) had, through the missionary superiors in Aleppo, assured him that a certain Maronite and a certain Melkite were professed Catholics, in consideration of which "they merit the protection of the Sacred Congregation ... in order to facilitate restitution of the many effects pirated from them by some Maltese corsairs."[56] Rome de-

[55] A. E., $B^1$1021, fols. 174-75, Poullard au Conseil de Marine, Seyde, 3/5/1720. Poullard's communication makes it clear of course that French merchants whose goods were carried by Syrians pressured the consuls to grant the Syrians these certificates. A dozen years later the ambassador, in discussing the "abuses" long connected with the issuance of these certificates, admitted the difficulty involved in resisting the pressure exerted in the Syrians' behalf by the French merchants (A. E., $B^1$405, unnumbered fols., de Villeneuve à Monsieur, Istanbul, 2/15/1732). He might also have noted the difficulty involved in resisting the pressures of Rome, the missionaries, and the Uniates themselves.

[56] Arch. Prop., *SC*, Vol. 1, fol. 316, Peleran à Messeigneurs, Alep, 7/29/1718, in French; see also the affidavit dated 7/30/1718, signed

cided, albeit nine years later, in favor of the offended Aleppines and compensation was paid.[57]

But quite apart from the question of restitution or compensation, the fact that these consular certificates did provide the Uniates with a wide margin of safety is confirmed by the alacrity with which Muslims and non-Uniate Christians placed their merchandise on vessels owned or operated by recipients of the consuls' grace; by the regularity with which Uniates shipped, under their own names and for a fee, merchandise owned by schismatics and infidels;[58] and by the emphasis placed upon these

---

by the Franciscan, Jesuit, and Carmelite superiors in Aleppo, and stating that the Maronite and Melkite in question are good Catholics who have, in fact, been plundered by the corsairs (*ibid.*, fol. 319, in Italian).

[57] See A. E., $B^1 81$, fols. 11-14, Pétition au Roi, 1729; *ibid.*, fols. 18-19, Peleran à [de Maurepas], Alep, 1/18/1729; *ibid.*, fols. 21-22 [Peleran's letter in support of the claims of Mas'ad and Masarrah], Alep, 1/17/1729; *ibid.*, Peleran à de Maurepas, Alep, 1/27/1730; *ibid.*, Peleran à [de Maurepas], Alep, 10/7/1730. The fact of Rome's regular interventions in behalf of Uniates plundered is noted by the French ambassador in Istanbul in 1730 (A. E., $B^1 401$, unnumbered fols., de Villeneuve à Monsieur, Istanbul, 4/12/1730).

[58] The French consul at Sidon in 1716 complained that the corsairs had taken to plundering the shipping of the French as well as that of the Uniates out of conviction that both groups, "to whom the consuls accord certificates . . . , lend their names to Turks in order to favor their [own] trade" (A. E., $B^1 1020$, fol. 58, Poullard Conseil de Marine, Seyde, 6/29/1716). Some three years later the same consul alluded to the tendency of the protected Christians to place, for a consideration, infidel cargo under their own names (A. E., $B^1 1021$, fol. 120, Poullard au Conseil de Marine, Seyde, 8/22/1719). The same propensity was noted by the consul at Aleppo in 1726 (A. E., $B^1 80$, fol. 191, Peleran à de Maurepas, Alep, 11/20/1726) and in 1730 by the ambassador, who pointed out the abuses long connected with these certificates (A. E., $B^1 401$, unnumbered fols., de Villeneuve à Monsieur, Istanbul, 4/12/1730).

certificates, and upon the entire question of protection against the corsairs, by Melkite prelates who had submitted, or were in the process of submitting, to Rome. Patriarch Cyril al-Zaʿīm's chronic concern with the problem of the corsairs is reflected in virtually all his correspondence with Rome and in his efforts to obtain papal intervention as part of the price for his own passage to the Unia.[59] And in a letter to the Propaganda, dated May 26, 1714, that most unequivocal of Uniates, Metropolitan Euthymius al-Ṣayfī of Sidon, for whose vessel the French consul had issued the very first certificate for protection against the corsairs,[60] did not hesitate to depict the European pirates as a decisive element in the ongoing struggle between fidelity and schism:

> As for your comment about removing from the Catholics the damages inflicted by the corsairs, it has much gladdened us, and many among the schismatics now incline their hearts toward acceptance of the Catholic faith. I used to grieve upon seeing a Catholic Christian reverting to his former infidelity and increasing in it because of his plunder by the corsairs. . . . Now, thank God, through your intervention . . . I have not lost a soul. To the contrary my gains are increased

[59] See, for example, Arch. Prop., *SOCG*, Vol. 608, fol. 149, Cyril to Biagio, 8/20/1716, in Arabic; *ibid.*, Vol. 625, fol. 481, Cyril to Sacripanti, Damascus, 9/1/1719, in Arabic; *ibid.*, fol. 486, Cyril to Clement XI, 9/1/1719, in Arabic; *ibid.*, fol. 495, Fīnān to Caraffa, 7/11/1719, in Arabic.

[60] "I have so far given only one certificate—to a saique which belongs to the bishop himself" (A. E., B$^1$1017, fol. 256, l'Empereur à [de Pontchartrain], Seyde, 3/23/1702).

and my witness concerning Catholics has become accepted by the corsairs themselves.[61]

The economic advantage imparted the Uniates by means of these consular certificates needs no further elaboration. What is far more important, however, is the extent to which these dispensations, together with the informal protection extended to Syrian Christians in the service of the French (and English) factories, abstracted these Ottoman subjects from the effective jurisdiction of the Ottoman government *long before* the widespread circulation of the *beret* of honorary dragoman. And the time had to come when the recipients of these certificates, and their more numerous fellows, the interpreter-agent-merchant and even the servants of Europeans, would press their patrons and the consuls for a formal patent of protection—at once broader and more closely defined and in some manner sanctioned by the Porte. It was in this way that the ubiquitous *beret* of honorary dragoman was to gain currency. Though initially the consuls, who after all were responsible for upholding these *berets*, were noticeably less enthusiastic about their issuance than were the European merchants whose dependence upon native protégés had not diminished with the passage of time, they, as well as the ambassadors, grew accustomed to the fees that accrued therefrom, and before the mid-eighteenth century the *beret* had become an established institution whose destructive impact on Ottoman urban society is not easily exaggerated. Seen in its proper perspective, therefore, the *beret* of honorary dragoman represented the formalization, by the Porte as well as the European powers, of privileges

[61] Arch. Prop., *SOCG*, Vol. 598, fol. 195, Euthymius to S. Congregation, 5/26/1714, in Arabic.

which were evolving during much of the seventeenth and early eighteenth century but with particular speed after 1680.

The same *ad hoc* system of patronage which spawned the *beret* of honorary dragoman, then, was instrumental in forging the Melkite schism. In a word, Rome and Catholic France could at last provide a large segment of the Syrian Christian élite with a protection more effective, and economic possibilities grander, than those associated with their ancestral *millet* and the Muslim imperium to which it was in half-bondage. For the Melkite bourgeoisie of Aleppo, Sidon, and Damascus—for decades exposed to Latin missionaries, and undergoing an era of increased prosperity which was closely related to the existence of French factories in Aleppo and Sidon and to the phenomenon of consular protection[62]—entry into the Unia repre-

[62] Although Damascus housed neither French consul nor factory, Sidon, which contained both, served as its port. On this basis it is reasonable to assume that many Damascene Melkite traders and merchants enjoyed close commercial and undoubtedly familial ties with their cosectaries on the coast, and hence were subject to some of the same religio-economic motivations. It is, for instance, unlikely that the constant preoccupation of the Damascus-domiciled Cyril al-Zaʿīm with the problem of the corsairs (above, p. 45 & n. 59) arose solely out of the patriarch's concern for his flock in Sidon. For the Melkites of Sidon had for decades paid far less deference to Cyril than to their refractory Uniate metropolitan, Euthymius al-Ṣayfī. Let it be observed in addition that the Uniates and missionaries in Damascus were extended the protection of the consul at Sidon and that his, as well as the ambassador's, interventions in their behalf were neither uncommon nor unsuccessful (A. E., $B^1$1017, fol. 240, ". . . lettres escrits . . . de Damas," 9/7 & 9/9/1701; A. E., $B^1$1018, fols. 36-37, Mémoire d'Estelle, 10/18/1704-3/2/1705; A. E., $B^1$77, fol. 254, L'Ambassadeur aux missionaires d'Alep, Istanbul, 1/28/1712; A. E., $B^1$1021, fol. 45, Poullard au Conseil de Marine, Seyde, 4/10/1719). Clearly, however, the more

sented a plausible response to the administrative and moral deterioration of the Patriarchate of Antioch and the gradual undermining of the Ottoman polity to which the Patriarchate was intimately bound. Of such was the stuff of schism; of such too the basis of one of the first substantial Western intrusions into a historic segment of Ottoman society.

That the Melkite rank and file, particularly in Aleppo and Sidon, fell in behind the Uniate bourgeoisie and clergy should occasion little surprise. Apart from the fact that the clergy were the legally constituted leaders of the community and the bourgeoisie their natural complement, the ordinary layman, in the absence of any clear unequivocal Orthodox opposition until the last years of the seventeenth century, was scarcely aware that a significant change was taking place. Until the formation of a Uniate patriarchate in 1724, the missionaries and their protégés were still working *within* the Orthodox Church. The Jesuits particularly (many well-versed in Arabic, frequently attired in the habit of Melkite priests and quite capable of blithely chanting the Eastern liturgy) went quietly about their task, studiously avoiding any overt attack on the Orthodox Church and believers.[63] In short,

---

modest gains of the Unia in Damascus, as contrasted to their virtually total success in Aleppo and Sidon, is in the main attributable to the absence of a French factory and consul.

[63] On the Jesuit practice of adopting the dress of native clergy so as to gain easier access to Syrian Christian homes, see Rabbath, II, 331, d'Andrezel au ministre, Istanbul, 7/23/1725; *ibid.*, II, 401, Fromage à un Jesuit Allemand, Antoura, 4/25/1730; *ibid.*, II, 401, n. 1. In general the missionaries avoided directly attacking the Orthodox Melkites until the relative apathy which had characterized the ecumenical patriarchate's attitude toward Latin proselytizing in Syria had been dispelled by the Synod of Constantinople,

no distinct Uniate ecclesiastical organization existed, and there was little outward sign that the Melkite Church of Antioch was undergoing radical transformation. The religious life of the rank and file continued more or less undisturbed by drastic innovation in liturgy or devotional practice; their duties and privileges remained largely unaffected; their socio-economic position, itself intimately connected with the bourgeoisie's level of prosperity, was if anything enhanced. It is important to note that the Unia claimed elements of the lower strata of the Melkite community only after they had won the lay and clerical élite; and that with few modifications the same process could be seen among the Armenian, Jacobite and Nestorian communities.

## VI

In the span of some one hundred years, then, the Latins succeeded in all but doubling the number of Syrian Churches and in destroying the tolerance and mutual accommodation which, on the eve of missionary penetration, seem to have characterized their relations. The bitterness and suspicion which stood between the Uniates and their parent Churches not infrequently erupted into violence in the eighteenth and nineteenth centuries and to this day has yet to be entirely dispelled. Any meaningful and consistent unity of action had been irretrievably lost.

The birth of the Uniate Melkite Church out of the bat-

---

1722. An Arabic translation of the *ekthesis* produced by this Synod is to be found in Biblioteca Apostolica Vaticana, *Vaticanus Arabicus*, MS 161. The text of the antimissionary *fermān* which the Synod succeeded in eliciting from the Porte in September 1722 is to be found in French translation in Rabbath, I, 546-47.

tered body of the Orthodox Patriarchate of Antioch was of particular moment for subsequent Syrian history. Where two Churches, the Maronite and Orthodox Melkite, had claimed the loyalty of upward of 90 percent of Syrian Christendom, there now stood three. And although the Orthodox maintained a numerical superiority over their Uniate kinsmen they lost to them some of their most élite elements. In wealth, education, and awareness of a world beyond the confines of the Ottoman Empire the Melkite bourgeoisie of Aleppo ranked second to no community within the Patriarchate and could compare favorably with any community of comparable size drawn from any sect in Syria. Nor were the defections in the thriving port of Sidon and the great entrepôt of Damascus losses which the Orthodox Melkites could easily sustain. The true extent of the damage became obvious as the Uniate Melkite migrations of the eighteenth century—inspired in part by Ottoman-Orthodox pressures but mainly by the economic decline which became endemic in Ottoman territories after 1750—carried the Uniates to several of the growing cities in the Lebanon,[64] to Ẓāhir al-'Umar's virtually independent principality of Acre,[65] and to the semi-

[64] See *below*, p. 60 & n. 81.

[65] Although the name of the Uniate Melkite, Ibrāhīm al-Ṣabbāgh, is indelibly linked with that of Ẓāhir al-'Umar (d. 1775), it is to be noted that for the better part of twenty years before the advent of Ibrāhīm, Ẓāhir's "*wazīr*" was another Uniate Melkite merchant called Yūsuf al-Qissīs (Mīkhā'īl al-Ṣabbāgh, *Ta'rīkh al-Shaykh Ẓāhir al-'Umar al-Zaydānī*, ed. Q. al-Bāshā [Ḥarīṣā, Lebanon, n.d.], p. 53). Other Uniate Melkites were prominent in Ẓāhir's administration, among them Mīkhā'īl al-Baḥrī (the father of Muḥammad 'Alī's celebrated minister, Ḥannā al-Baḥrī), Sim'ān al-Ṣabbāgh—a priest fluent in Arabic, Greek and French—who played a significant role in the negotiations which led to Ẓāhir's

autonomous Egypt of the revived Mamlūk Beys,[66] there to occupy primary positions in internal and external trade and in the counsels and financial administrations of these and other local rulers who rose to fill the vacuum left by the fading authority of the Ottoman central government. Not unnaturally the Uniate Melkites sought out those areas governed by men who, like themselves, stood outside full Ottoman legality; and there their commercial talents, European connections, and the linguistic skills acquired through these connections and through the Uniate seminaries of the Lebanon assured them a warm reception.

By tipping the scales of Syrian Christianity in favor of the Unia and their European patrons, the Melkite schism had yet broader implications for Syrian society in general. It is to make no exaggerated claims for the extent and depth of their understanding of the West to remark that until well into the twentieth century the Uniate Melkites were the most "westernized" Arabic-speaking com-

---

brief alliance with the Russians, and Yūsuf al-Ṣabbāgh (Ibrāhīm's son) who was secretary to Ẓāhir's governor at Jaffa (*ibid.*, pp. 27, 121, 133).

[66] In 1763 the Mamlūk, 'Alī Bey, seized the office of *shaykh al-balad* and shortly thereafter conferred the customs farm of Egypt, hitherto held by Jews, upon a Uniate Melkite. Save for one brief interruption Uniate Melkites retained control until the last years of Mamlūk rule. And by the time they were obliged to yield the customs farm to the personal administration of Murād Bey the loss had little meaning. Their years as customs farmers had given the Uniate Melkites first rank in Egyptian commerce as well as a virtual monopoly over European consular positions in Egypt (*ibid.*, pp. 90-91; Paul Carali [Būluṣ Qara'lī], *Les Syriens en Égypte*, Vol. 1: *Au Temps des Mamluks* [Égypte, n.d.], pp. 85-86, in Arabic; Qusṭanṭīn al-Bāshā, *Muḥāḍarah fī Ta'rīkh Ṭā'ifah al-Rūm al-Kāthūlīk fī Miṣr* [Ḥarīṣā, Lebanon, n.d.], pp. 14-16, 33, 35-36, 42).

munity in Syria (and Egypt) and the most alienated from indigenous traditions and values. Even after they received Ottoman recognition as a distinct community in 1839 the Uniate Melkites remained a singular community in Syrian society, drawing perhaps the greater part of their moral, intellectual, and material sustenance from their European associations.

There was a touch of paradox as well as tragedy in this situation. For it had been Uniate Melkites as well as Maronites who, in the early eighteenth century, produced the first halting attempts to carry the linguistic Arabization of the Syrian Christians beyond the ecclesiastical and into the realm of profane literature. Niqūlā al-Ṣā'igh (1692-1756), his cousin 'Abdallāh Zākhir, the Maronite Germanos Farḥāt and other Uniates had dominated that remarkable group of Uniate Aleppines who, having availed themselves of the Latin mission schools, as well as the more humble primary schools maintained by their respective communities, ventured a thorough study of classical Arabic under a Muslim *shaykh*.[67] Not only was a new linguistic respectability imparted through their efforts to subsequent Arabic translations of Greek, Latin, and Syriac ecclesiastical works but a new impetus was given both to the production of historical chronicles which did not dwell exclusively on Church history, and, most significantly, to Christian incursions into Arabic poetry in the classical forms.[68]

[67] On this Aleppine group see Graf, III, 187-207, 406-28; L. Shaykhū, "Tarjamah al-Ṭayyib al-Athar al-Khūrī Nīqūlāwus al-Ṣā'igh," *Al-Machriq*, VI (1903), 99-100; P. Bacel, "Nicholas Saïgh, religieux chouérite, 1692-1756," *Echos d'Orient*, XI (March 1908), 72-73.

[68] Of the Aleppine group the most important contributions to

Simultaneously, long and increasingly closer contact with resident European traders who came not simply as Christians but as French, English, Dutch, and Venetians, together with long exposure to the missions which if staffed by religious were yet staffed by Westerners,[69] had introduced, in however rudimentary a fashion, the European ethno-linguistic concept of "nation." It was indicative of this sharpened ethnic awareness that a Uniate Melkite notable of Damascus could phrase his protest against the ecumenical patriarchate's unilateral designation of an ethnic Greek to the throne of Antioch in 1724 less in terms of the faithful's revulsion against heresy than in those of an Arab reaction to Greek encroachments. Insisting (inaccurately) that "from the Ottoman conquest to the present . . . our patriarch had always been an Arab from among us . . . ," the Damascene concluded that the recent usurpation clearly indicated "the intentions of the Greeks of Istanbul to extend their hand over the Arabs. . . ."[70]

While it would not do to exaggerate the extent of either the Arabic literary revival or the assimilation of the Eu-

---

Arabic poetry were made by Germanos Farḥāt and Niqūlā al-Ṣā'igh; on the work of the latter see Graf, III, 201-207; on that of the former, *ibid.*, III, 406-28.

[69] The feuding between the usually Spanish and Italian Franciscans on one hand and the largely French Jesuits and Capuchins was apparent at least as early as the 1670's and, some seventy years later, had scarcely diminished. Nor is there any question that differences among the missionaries were grounded in their different political loyalties (see A. E., B¹76, fol. 42, Dupont au Ministre, Alep, 5/?/1677; *ibid.*, fol. 42 [a letter written by the Jesuits in Aleppo]; *ibid.*, fol. 359, Blanc à de Pontchartrain, Alep, 12/10/1698; Rabbath, II, 573-74, Mémoire du Marquis de Villeneuve, 1740).

[70] Arch. Prop., *SC*, Vol. II, fol. 78, Manṣūr Ṣayfī [*sic*] to S. Congregation, Damascus, 1/20/1728, in Arabic.

ropean idea of "nation," even in their nebulous forms they mark a turning point in the development of the ethnic consciousness upon which the Arabic-speaking Near East would be to some degree reorganized as the primacy of the religious identity was questioned and slowly and painfully (and today still quite incompletely) abandoned. The paradox of the Uniate Melkite role in this awakening lies in the fact that the Syrian-Arab ethnic awareness they helped initially to foster was to receive fullest development, at least among Christians, in the Orthodox Melkite community.

The confusion of identity which tore the Uniate Melkites from the outset, and which has yet to be wholly resolved, received its initial expression in the struggle between the Latinizing and anti-Latinizing factions of the community. We have observed that one of the strengths of the missionary effort was its emphasis on maintaining virtually unaltered the rites and practices of each Syrian Church, thereby minimizing the difficulties of passage to the Unia. This view corresponded nicely to that held by the Melkite members of the Uniate literary coterie in Aleppo who, having matured before open schism placed them beyond Ottoman legality and before the shadow of Europe had been cast so broadly over the Near East, could retain an unself-conscious pride in their specifically Eastern heritage. Indeed, their forays into Arabic literature represented one aspect of their attempt to come to grips with their tradition.

Concurrently, however, an opposing tendency was at work. If the anti-Latinizing faction of the Uniate Melkites was strong at Aleppo and among the Shwayrite monastic community founded and supported by Aleppines, the Latinizing faction had its stronghold in Sidon and among the Salvatorian Congregation founded by that city's metropolitan, Euthymius al-Ṣayfī (d. 1723).[71] For their part the Uniate Melkites of Damascus seem to have been evenly divided although some members of the Latinizing faction were sufficiently extreme to desire total absorption by the Latin rite.[72] It was a minor disaster for the defenders of Eastern tradition that the first Uniate Melkite patriarch, Cyril al-Ṭānās (1724-1760), a nephew of al-Ṣayfī, was a Salvatorian monk imbued with the Latinizing tendencies of his monastic congregation and its founder.[73] Shortly be-

[71] In a letter to the Propaganda, written before his reversion to Orthodoxy, Patriarch Athanasius al-Dabbās tells of the strife occasioned by the Latinizing policies of Euthymius, "our brother" (Arch. Prop., *SC*, Vol. I, fols. 368-69, Athanasius to S. Congregation, Damascus, 1720, in Arabic); and in a letter written in the same year by a Uniate Melkite monk warns the Propaganda that abandonment of the traditional Eastern rites and fasts is giving rise to serious problems within the community (*ibid.*, fol. 409, 'Āṭallāh to S. Congregation, 8/17/1720, in Arabic). Al-Ṣayfī's defense rested upon a characteristic premise of the Latinizers—the necessity of ridding the Eastern Church of all "innovation," however sanctified by time and tradition, "for, as regards the sons of the East, unity in faith is in itself insufficient; they must abandon all practices innovated and intruded upon them by the heretics" (*ibid.*, fol. 402, Euthymius to Clement XI, Sidon, August 1720, in Arabic).

[72] See Arch. Prop., *SC*, Vol. II, fol. 414, "The Catholics" [of Damascus] to S. Congregation, 12/1/1731, in Arabic; *ibid.*, fol. 417, "The Damascene Catholics" to S. Congregation, 12/1/1731, in Arabic; *ibid.*, Vol. III, fol. 96, "The Latins of the Damascene Greek Community" to Zondadari, 11/27/1734, in Arabic; *ibid.*, Vol. IV, fols. 24-25, "The Damascene Christians" to S. Congregation, 7/15/1739), in Arabic.

[73] Niqūlā al-Ṣā'igh, himself a Shwayrite monk and intent upon upholding Eastern usage, was for years one of the more powerful protestors against the Latinizing policies of Cyril al-Ṭānās (*ibid.*,

fore his death Cyril sought to perpetuate his policy by designating his great-nephew, Athanasius Jawhar, as his successor. Rome's rejection of Jawhar's succession did not derive wholly from its irregular aspect. It was inspired in large measure by papal concern for preserving Eastern Church tradition in face of the encroachments of the Latin rite and canons.[74] Rome, however, never fully comprehended that the Ottoman-Orthodox view of the Uniate Melkites as "Franks" was in a sense shared by many of the Uniate Melkite bourgeoisie and hierarchy themselves; that membership in the Unia, which Rome saw as the means of restoring the religious unity of East and West in all its ancient variety, was seen by an ever-increasing number of Uniates as part of the process of Europeanization. (It was not merely a taste for hyperbole that had prompted al-Ṣayfī to write to Louis XIV in 1706 assuring him that "though our necks be bent under the yoke of the Muslims, we regard ourselves only as *your* subjects. . . .")[75]

Rome remained formally committed to upholding Eastern tradition; indeed throughout the eighteenth and much

---

Vol. II, fol. 522, Niqūlā to Yūsuf, 8/20/1732, in Arabic). Nor was al-Ṣā'igh's cousin, the deacon 'Abdallāh Zākhir, less adamant in his efforts to preserve Eastern tradition (*ibid.*, fol. 532, Zākhir to Manṣūr, 8/17/1732, in Arabic). For al-Ṭānās' defense, see *ibid.*, fol. 526, Cyril to Clement XII, 8/29/1732, in Arabic; *ibid.*, fol. 537, Cyril to S. Congregation, 9/1/1732, in Arabic.

[74] It was no mistake that Rome's candidate was Maximos Ḥakīm, a member of the old Aleppine literary coterie and a Shwayrite monk who shared his congregation's aversion to Latinization. Ḥakīm's succession represented the apogee of traditionalists' influence in the eighteenth century. Their triumph, however, was short-lived.

[75] A. E., $B^1$1018, fol. 325, Euthymius au Roi, Seyde, 9/27/1706, in Arabic; a French translation is to be found in Rabbath, II, 410.

of the nineteenth century only the interventions of Rome stood between the Uniates and wholesale Latinization.[76] But she was never able to control completely the opposing tendency, particularly as the accelerated Western penetration which commenced in the latter half of the eighteenth century brought into question the whole of Eastern traditions and values. The Uniate Melkite clergy, trained by Latins in Syria and Rome; and the bourgeoisie, educated in the mission schools, pursuing trade to the great ports of Europe and (after the mid-eighteenth century) enjoying not infrequently one variety or other of European nationality, became in the course of the nineteenth century almost totally oriented toward the West. An essentially middle-class community possessing considerable economic power, and in prolonged and intimate contact with the civilization whose institutions were to undermine utterly those of the Near East, the Uniate Melkites, with only individual exceptions, came to constitute not a bridge between Europe and their homeland but a classic Levantine community consciously at work disowning much of its

[76] For examples drawn from the eighteenth century, see Arch. Prop., *CP*, Vol. 75, fols. 304-305, al-Ṭānās to S. Congregation, 2/20/1723, in Arabic; Arch. Prop., *SC*, Vol. 11, fol. 417, "The Damascene Catholics" to S. Congregation, Damascus, 12/1/1731, in Arabic; *ibid.*, fol. 522, Niqūlā to Yūsuf, 8/20/1732, in Arabic; A. E., B¹83, fols. 11-12, de Lane à Monseigneur, Alep, 2/1/1737; A. E., B¹84, fols. 342-44, Aubergy à de Maurepas (?), Alep, 8/3/1745; A. E., B¹87, fols. 223-24, Thomas à Monseigneur, Alep, 7/2/1756. The papal position is enshrined in Benedict XIV's bull, *Demandatam*, dated 12/24/1743. Although Cyril al-Ṭānās indicated his adhesion to this bull in October 1744 (see Arch. Prop., *CP*, Vol. 83, fols. 308-16 [text of *Demandatam* in Latin and Arabic, bearing Cyril's signature]), the Latinizing patriarch honored it most commonly in the breach.

peculiarly Eastern heritage and trying to be, though it could never quite be, Western. Nor was this development arrested with Ottoman recognition of the Uniate Melkites as a separate community in 1839, a step which was correctly viewed by the neophytes as further tribute to the European power which had been their refuge.

## VII

In terms of deepening attachment to and dependence on Rome and the patronage of France, the development of the Maronite community in the eighteenth century differed from that of the Uniate Melkites only in degree. A concordat with the papacy was concluded in 1736, only four years before the Capitulations of 1740 legalized the *de facto* situation by forbidding Ottoman officialdom to molest Frenchmen (and most of the missionaries *were* Frenchmen) and tributary subjects of the Sultan in their dealings with one another.[77] The fact that from 1655 to 1758 France drew her consuls in Beirut from the Maronite Khāzin family is additional testimony to the intimacy of the Maronite-French connection.[78] Meanwhile the basis for Maronite political preeminence in the Lebanon was taking shape.

The hegemony of the Druzes, that extremely heterodox Muslim sect occupying the southern portion of the Lebanon, had been established in the early seventeenth century. For reasons still not altogether clear, however, the

[77] *Above*, p. 31 & n. 36.

[78] Although not to any advantage accruing thereby to the French factories—as witness the complaints of the consul at Sidon in 1704 concerning the incumbent Khāzin's lack of effectiveness (A. E., $B^1$1017, fol. 398, Mémoire de Stelle [*sic*], Seyde, 5/2/1704).

seventeenth and eighteenth centuries witnessed a steady migration of Maronite and to a lesser extent Orthodox Melkite peasantry from the northern reaches of the Mountain into the Druze districts of the south. By the middle of the eighteenth century the Druzes were reduced to a minority—albeit a politically dominant minority—in their traditional territory. The position of the Druze feudal aristocracy was further undermined by a propensity for internecine strife; and before 1750 three Maronite shaykhly families had achieved equality of feudal rank with the five paramount Druze houses of the Lebanon.

However, the Muslim princely house of al-Shihāb had been dominant in the Mountain since the turn of the century, their Sunnī Islam serving both to calm somewhat the Ottoman sensibility and place them in the role of referee between contending Druze factions. The conversion (beginning in 1756) of the more important elements of the house of al-Shihāb to Maronite Christianity was a symbol of the new forces transforming the traditional polity of the Lebanon.[79] For the apostasy of these alleged descendants from the tribe of the Prophet reflected not only the growing Maronite preponderance and the Druze decline but the steadily slackening grip of the Sunnī Ottoman authority. Though Druze hegemony was not to be entirely undone until the latter half of the nineteenth century the movement of Maronites into the south continued apace and with it the expansion of Maronite influence throughout the Mountain.

[79] On the decline of Druze and the rise of Maronite fortunes in this period, see W. R. Polk, *The Opening of South Lebanon, 1788-1840* (Cambridge, Mass., 1963); I. F. Harik, *Politics and Change in a Traditional Society: Lebanon, 1711-1845* (Princeton, 1968); Salibi, pp. 5-14.

The arrival in the Lebanon during the eighteenth and early nineteenth century of Uniate Melkites from Aleppo and Damascus also strengthened the Maronite hand as well as the overall position of the Unia in Syrian affairs. While the Maronites complemented their growing political strength by achieving ascendancy in the production of silk (the most important industry of the Lebanon),[80] Uniate Melkite merchants tightened their hold over the Syro-Egyptian coastal trade and, to some extent, the traffic with Europe, even as other of their cosectaries, newly arrived from the interior, were creating the modern towns of Zaḥlah and Dayr al-Qamr, the former emerging as the center of communications connecting Damascus and the fertile Biqāʿ valley to the expanding port of Beirut, and the latter as the seat of the now Christian Shihābī *amīrs*.[81]

Nor was the Uniate Melkite influence confined to the economic and (at least indirectly) the political realms. Men like al-Ṣā'igh and Zākhir, the one with his poetry and ecclesiastical literature, the other with his Arabic press, sought refuge in the Maronite districts. In conjunction with the Latin schools in the Lebanon and Rome, and the occasional efforts of Uniate monasteries to provide education for the laity, al-Ṣā'igh and Zākhir elevated the general level of learning and quickened the Arabic

[80] *Ibid.*, p. 12.

[81] Burckhardt, in 1810, saw in the mountain town of Zaḥlah five Uniate Melkite churches, one monastery and a population he estimated at 5000 souls. According to the same traveler the population was almost entirely Uniate Melkite, had more than quadrupled in the past twenty-five years and was still growing (J. L. Burckhardt, *Travels in Syria and the Holy Land* [London, 1822], p. 5). On the movement of Uniate Melkites to the Lebanon, see al-Bāshā, *Muḥāḍarah*, p. 8 & n. 2, pp. 9, 11.

literary revival nurtured originally by them and other Uniates in Aleppo. Not a few of the Uniate Melkites who came to control much of the commerce of Syria and Egypt, as well as the financial administrations of the semiautonomous local rulers who emerged from the political wreckage of the eighteenth and early nineteenth century, received their education in the Latin and Uniate establishments of the Lebanon.[82] It should be noted parenthetically that the Christian element in the Mountain population with least access to education of any kind was the Orthodox Melkite.

The accelerated pace of the Arabic literary revival was reflected most significantly in the chronicles which made their appearance in some number around the turn of the eighteenth century and helped lay a historical basis for an incipient Lebanese nationalism. The notion of the Lebanon as a distinct political unit was, of course, not without grounding in geography and historical fact. Since time immemorial its relative isolation and heterodox population had given rise to varying degrees of political autonomy *vis-à-vis* the "orthodox" government that controlled the rest of Syria. Even in the era of maximum Ottoman power the Druze *amīr* Fakhr al-Dīn (d. 1635) had succeeded, with the support of the Maronites, in carving out a virtually independent principality with a Lebanese nucleus. Maronite history, moreover, was almost wholly centered in the rugged terrain of the Mountain; and when, inspired by the literary revival of the late seven-

[82] Ibrāhīm al-Ṣabbāgh, the "*wazīr*" of Ẓāhir al-ʿUmar (*see above*, p. 50, n. 65), was among the prominent Uniate Melkites who were educated at the hands of the Shwayrite Congregation and their abbot, Niqūlā al-Ṣā'igh (see L. Shaykhū, "Mīkhā'īl al-Ṣabbāgh wa Usratuhu," *Al-Machriq*, VIII [1905], 25-26).

teenth and early eighteenth century, Maronites turned once again to a study of their own Church they could not but see it largely in the context of their historic homeland. Whatever his intent, when Isṭifānūs al-Duwayhī (1629-1704), graduate of the Maronite College in Rome and after 1670 Maronite patriarch, authored his history of the Maronites, he brought forth a work which was not less a history of the Lebanon than were the later profane chronicles of Ḥaydar al-Shihābī (1761-1835) and Ṭannūs al-Shidyāq (1794-1861).[83]

In an age which was gradually assuming the primacy of the ethno-linguistic identity the Maronites, of all Syrians, were burdened with least ambivalence. Though, as we shall see, some of them were to entertain the idea of a more broadly based Syrian or Arab polity, and though they never lost their sense of community with Catholic Christendom, their specifically Maronite religious identity was virtually indistinguishable from their Lebanese identity. No other sect in Syria, Christian or Muslim, was characterized by a comparable equation. To a marked degree, of course, this peculiarly Lebanese sentiment of the Maronites obtained among the Uniate Melkites of Lebanon as well. As a community, however, their much wider geographic distribution throughout Syria (not to mention Egypt) and their greater dependence on European—or in any case extra-Lebanese sources of authority—stood between them and the totally Lebanese view which came to prevail among the Maronites. The situation of the Orthodox Melkites was still more complex.

[83] See Isṭifānūs al-Duwayhī, *Ta'rīkh al-Azminah* (Beirut, 1951); al-Shihābī, *Al-Ghurar*; Ṭannūs al-Shidyāq, *Kitāb Akhbār al-A'yān fī Jabal Lubnān* (Beirut, 1859).

## VIII

For the Orthodox Melkites of Syria the period from roughly 1725 to 1850 was a time of recovery from the trauma of schism. Since most of their lay and clerical élite had passed to the Unia it was largely under the control of Greek prelates appointed directly by the ecumenical see that a partial recovery was effected. The emergence of the Uniate Melkites was the primary factor inspiring the Patriarchate of Constantinople to abandon its policy of occasional and usually ill-advised intervention in the affairs of the Antiochian see for one of direct control through the agency of a Greek hierarchy foisted upon the Syrians without reference to the latter's wishes. Greek control was not without its weaknesses. In administrative integrity the Greeks represented no great improvement over the Syrians. Their maximum effectiveness, moreover, was confined to those places where officials of the Ottoman central government were capable of, and disposed toward, enforcing their decisions; and, as the eighteenth century wore on, such areas became fewer and fewer. We have seen that in the wake of Ottoman decline, local forces which had always conditioned contacts between the Syrians and the central government assumed a new strength and vitality. "All over the Empire, there arose local ruling groups controlling the machinery of local Government, ultimately loyal to the Sultan but possessing a force, a stability, and to some degree an autonomy of their own."[84] And as a natural corollary they displayed a willingness to use and protect those elements whose position in relation to the Ottoman government was as irregular

[84] A. Hourani, *A Vision of History* (Beirut, 1961), p. 47.

as their own, and whose commercial and bureaucratic skills and European connections could be turned to advantage. The Lebanese *amīrs*, Ẓāhir al-ʿUmar at Acre, the Mamlūk Beys and later Muḥammad ʿAlī in Egypt, and to a lesser extent the al-ʿAẓms of Damascus were not to be expected to view the Uniate Melkites in light of Ottoman definitions which held them to be extralegal.[85] The Uniates were simply too valuable to be lightly dismissed.

Nonetheless the Greek hierarchy in Syria could at least be certain that in any confrontation with the Uniate Melkites they would be upheld by the Great Church and central government on a less irregular and far less expensive basis than their Syrian predecessors had been. This fact was not lost on the Syrians; and until the latter half of the nineteenth century the Greeks were acknowledged by the great majority of their Syrian flock as the best hope for order within the patriarchate and for defense against Uniate penetration. It has only to be added that Greek immunity to papal overtures was well-nigh complete.

But if the Syrians were to suffer the Greeks until the last decade of the nineteenth century, as years passed they

[85] *Above*, pp. 50-51 & nn. 65, 66. Imperial orders notwithstanding, the treatment accorded the Uniate Melkites of Damascus by Asʿad Pasha al-ʿAẓm was not discernibly different from that accorded the Orthodox (Mīkhāʾīl Burayk, *Taʾrīkh al-Shām, 1720-1782*, ed. Q. al-Bāshā [Ḥarīṣā, Lebanon, 1930], pp. 16, 19). Nor is it necessary to dismiss Burayk's allegations that Asʿad received sizable bribes from the Uniate Melkites (*ibid.*) before suggesting that, given the local roots of al-ʿAẓm authority, the Pasha's true imperative was to end the endemic strife which tore the majority element among the Damascene *dhimmīs*. It is to be noted that the alleged bribes did not keep the Orthodox chronicler from paying tribute to Asʿad's sense of justice (*ibid.*, pp. 11, 13).

did so less and less gladly. For even as Ottoman hostility and (more to the point) European patronage were slowly transforming the Uniate Melkites from a community secure in its Eastern Church traditions and showing at least faint glimmers of a Syrian-Arab national awareness into a community largely alienated from its historic milieu, the Orthodox Melkites were acquiring something of that awareness which was being aborted in their Uniate brethren. A number of related factors accounted for this. In the first place the Orthodox Melkites lacked a European patron as firmly committed to them as France to the Uniates—the influence of Orthodox Russia was not felt in Syria until the second half of the nineteenth century nor was it thereafter comparable in depth or extent to that wielded by the French.[86] At the same time the Orthodox of Syria were not oblivious to the ethnic and linguistic criteria which divided resident Europeans, not excluding those carriers of a universalist faith, the Latin missionaries. Moreover the ecclesiastical control of Greeks who, not unaffected by the nationalist virus making its way eastward into the Balkans, tended more and more frequently to come as Greeks rather than as Orthodox, slowly fostered a Syrian reaction. (It might be noted in this regard that language revival and aversion to Greek ecclesiastical control were two cornerstones of early Balkan nationalism.) Though it did not achieve rank as a standing affront until the mid-nineteenth century, the changing Greek attitude could be seen as early as the 1760's when a Syrian candidate for the patriarchal succession was summarily rejected by the ecumenical see

[86] *Below*, pp. 83-85.

"lest some one of the Arabs come in and . . . extinguish the bright flame of Orthodoxy."[87]

The decline of the Ottoman authority, to which the Greek administration was inextricably bound, also helped foster the ethnic awareness of the Syrians (indeed of all the Sultan's subjects) by obliging them to turn to local institutions and local rulers for self-protection. This, of course, was no less true of the Maronites and Uniate Melkites. But whereas the Maronites were concentrated in the Lebanon; and the Uniate Melkites (their leadership particularly) were strongly represented, not only in Aleppo and Damascus but in precisely those areas enjoying widest autonomy and most susceptible to Western influence—that is, in Acre, Egypt, and the Mountain; the Orthodox Melkites retained their greatest strength in areas usually less autonomous and relatively unexposed to the European impact. Yet, while it is certain that 'Abdallāh al-Yāzijī, the Orthodox governor of Ḥimṣ in the 1750's under the only mildly autonomous pasha of Damascus, As'ad al-'Aẓm,[88] saw himself as more fully an Ottoman subject than did Ibrāhīm al-Ṣabbāgh, the Uniate

[87] From the document announcing the ecumenical patriarchate's unilateral election of Daniel the Chiot to the throne of Antioch, an English translation of which document is to be found in J. M. Neale, *A History of the Holy Eastern Church: the Patriarchate of Antioch* (London, 1873), pp. 193-94.

[88] The first of the al-Yāzijī family to serve the al-'Aẓms were Yūsuf and Ni'mah, both of whom were employed as *kātibs* by Ismā'īl al-'Aẓm, governor of Damascus from 1725 to 1730 (Burayk, *Ta'rīkh*, p. 7). During much of the time that 'Abdallāh al-Yāzijī served As'ad al-'Aẓm, his brother Ilyās was the *kahyā* (steward) of As'ad's brother, Sa'd al-Dīn (Rūfā'īl Karāmah, *Maṣādir Ta'rīkhīyah li Ḥawādith Lubnān wa Sūrīyā*, ed. B. Qaṭṭan [Beirut, 1929], p. 10).

Melkite minister of the virtually independent governor of Acre, Ẓāhir al-'Umar, it is unlikely that 'Abdallāh would have defined his relationship to the Sultan or his ethnic and religious identity in terms which an Orthodox a century before would fully have comprehended.

For the Orthodox Melkites of 'Abdallāh's era there was instruction in the fact that As'ad Pasha had permitted them to dress in any colors (other than the Prophet's green) which suited them, to imbibe their beloved *'araq* and wine openly in public gardens and baths, and to circulate publicly with a freedom (the Orthodox Melkite chronicler assures us) "never enjoyed by their ancestors nor ever to be enjoyed by their posterity."[89] In contrast the brief restoration of direct Ottoman authority not only aborted the *dhimmī* experiment in public display but resulted in the imprisonment of the patriarch and heavy fines for building a church where allegedly none stood before. Significantly too the deposition of As'ad al-'Aẓm led 'Abdallāh al-Yāzijī to seek refuge in the monasteries of the Lebanon where a rapid conversion to the Unia provided the erstwhile Orthodox champion with the key to high place in the service of the Lebanese *amīrs*.[90] It is not entirely irrelevant that the phrase, "may God make him victorious," which the mid-seventeenth century Orthodox Melkite chronicler, Paul of Aleppo, regularly affixed to the name of the Sultan, is conspicuously absent in the late eighteenth-century chronicle of Mīkhā'īl Burayk.[91] One

[89] Burayk, *Ta'rīkh*, p. 63.

[90] *Ibid.*, pp. 64-66; Karāmah, p. 22. 'Abdallāh was no doubt quick to realize that under the *amīrs*, as under Ẓāhir al-'Umar, only Uniates could aspire to a position comparable to that which he had enjoyed under the al-'Aẓms.

[91] Būlus al-Za'īm, p. 108 *et passim*.

wonders, moreover, whether Paul, thrust suddenly into the age of Burayk, would have paused with his Damascene cosectary to note that the al-'Aẓms were Arabs[92] or whether he would have instinctively dismissed the ethnic and linguistic differences which separated them from other Ottoman governors as no more noteworthy than those which distinguished his father, Patriarch Macarius, from his Greek predecessor on the throne of Antioch.[93] Clearly, a situation which found a Syrian patriarchal candidate opposed by Greek prelates on grounds that he was an "Arab"[94] would have introduced Paul to values antithetical to those which pervaded his well-ordered Ottoman world—a world inhabited by Muslims and Christians and only secondarily by Turks, Arabs, and Greeks. At all events Greek ecclesiastical control was one among several factors which, until its elimination in 1898, served to heighten Syrian-Arab awareness among the Orthodox Melkites.

## IX

Like most of the round and powerless world in the nineteenth century, Syria underwent revolutionary change. The Egyptian occupation (1832-1840) put an end to the political fragmentation of Syria (though the Lebanon, as

[92] Burayk, *Ta'rīkh*, p. 36.

[93] That Patriarch Euthymius (1635-47) was a Chiot from the monastery of Mār Sābā inspired no more resentment among the Syrian faithful than had the election of an "Arab" patriarch to the see of Alexandria, among the predominantly Greek faithful, some one hundred years before (see Makāriyūs al-Za'īm, fols. 127, 130; Būlus al-Za'īm, p. 43; Burayk, *Asāmī*, fol. 134).

[94] Burayk, *Ta'rīkh*, p. 75; *above*, pp. 65-66 & n. 87.

always, managed to retain much of its own counsel); opened the coastal areas to an unprecedented wave of European traders, travelers, and missionaries; and effected the *de jure* emancipation of Syrian Christians from the discriminatory aspects of Muslim law.[95] If Muḥammad ʿAlī's solicitude for Christians was on one level merely an effort to gain the acquiescence of Europe in his expansionist ambitions and place him in happy contrast to the Ottoman Sultan, it also represented the first tacit admission by a powerful Muslim head of state that the Islamic definitions of citizenship were unequal to the tasks at hand. The great Ottoman reform edicts of 1839 and 1856 merely echoed this conclusion and ushered in the policy of "Ottomanization," that ill-fated attempt to reconstruct Ottoman polity in terms which would allow for the participation of non-Muslims on that level of equality denied them by the sacred law.

As the Hapsburgs had come to appreciate, however, it was not a century for multinational empires. The policy of Ottomanization served to arrest not at all the already powerful Balkan nationalisms in reply to which it had been devised; and by the last quarter of the nineteenth century the Ottoman Empire consisted almost exclusively of the heavily Muslim Turkish and Arabic-speaking territories of the Near East. On the eve of the twentieth

[95] An authentic glimpse of the quite predictable reactions of Muslim and non-Muslim Damascenes to Ibrāhīm Pasha's order that "all Jews and Christians be placed in all respects on an equal footing with Moslems [*sic*], being permitted to ride in and about the city, and to wear white turbans" is to be obtained from the contemporary account of the Orthodox Melkite, Asʿad Khayyāṭ (Assaad Y. Kayat, *A Voice from the Lebanon* [London, 1847], pp. 88, 263-65).

century Ottomanization would have little meaning except in terms of Turko-Arab federation. In the wake of the destruction of the theoretic Islamic theocracy the Near East groped for new principles of social and political organization.

## X

We have observed that the capacity of the marginal community to influence and shape has been greatest at those times when the characteristic institutions of the dominant community were in the process of formation, radical modification, or destruction. All three conditions were met in the Islamic Near East in the nineteenth century, giving the Syrian Christian an opportunity for decisive influence which had not been his for a millennium. As once he had delivered up to the Muslim conqueror the Hellenistic treasure, he helped now to transmit to the Muslim vanquished the modern European learning which alone seemed capable of reviving him. But if during the first age of transmission the Christian's role had been confined to posing questions which Islam was compelled to answer, and which answered served inevitably to formalize the Christian's marginality, his role now was to share in phrasing the answers which promised him finally an end to the burden of marginality. The Christian's ability to influence and shape derived of course from his now complete linguistic Arabization, his longer exposure and easier access to the West, and his own immense stake in developing social and political institutions in which he could fully participate.

The Arabic literary revival among Christians in the

eighteenth and the first half of the nineteenth century had produced in its ecclesiastical aspect translations and apologetics, and in its profane aspect historical chronicles, and poetry which aimed at nothing beyond imitation of the classical models. The keynote had been rediscovery rather than invention. This tendency reached its fullest development in the work of the Uniate Melkite Nāṣīf al-Yāzijī (1800-1871), perhaps the nineteenth century's outstanding practitioner of classical Arabic. His poetry, however, despite its extraordinary virtuosity broke little fresh ground. This further development was to be the privilege of al-Yāzijī's friend and colleague Buṭrus al-Bustānī (1819-1882), whose dictionary, encyclopedia, and experiments in periodical literature were to influence much of subsequent Arabic prose and journalism.[96] Before the last quarter of the nineteenth century even Muslims were obliged to acknowledge the accomplishment and inventiveness of certain Christians in the language of the Koran. *For the marginal community at or above the cultural level of the dominant group, invention, with its possibilities for undermining the order which had pronounced it marginal, is a natural impulse.* For the Muslim to tamper with classical Arabic was to tamper with the tongue in which was framed the final and perfect Revelation, the tongue which was inseparably connected with the thought and institutions which had assured his dominance. For

[96] For an evaluation of al-Yāzijī and al-Bustānī, see A. Hourani, *Arabic Thought in the Liberal Age* (Oxford, 1967), pp. 95, 99-102; A. L. Tibawi, "The American Missionaries in Beirut and Butrus al-Bustani," *St. Antony's Papers, Number 16, Middle Eastern Affairs* (London, 1963), pp. 137-82. On the works of al-Yāzijī, see Graf, IV, 318-23 *et passim*; of al-Bustānī, *ibid.*, IV, 326-27 *et passim*.

the Christian, invention in Arabic was bound by no such inhibitions; to the contrary it was an unconscious means of constructing a new order to which he could lay equal claim.

By 1875 a number of related and no less significant developments had taken place, not the least of which was the arrival and early development of the Protestant missions, mainly American, on Lebanese soil. These missions, which acquired their foothold during the comparative security of the well-policed Egyptian occupation had little success in persuading Uniates and non-Uniates of the error of their ways. It was not simply that they arrived in an age when the primacy of the religious identity was already being questioned by the few. Unlike the Latins who, in formal religious terms, demanded little beyond submission to Rome, the Protestants struck at the heart of the ecclesiastical organization and the devotional life of the Eastern Christians. So little, initially, had rites and canons been altered by the Latins that most of their neophytes had passed to the Unia with scarcely any awareness that they had done so. The Protestant demand was of an entirely different nature and hardly calculated to have a broad appeal. But the importance of the Protestant missionaries is to be measured less in the number than in the quality of at least their early converts, and in the educational facilities provided, which (to the general advantage) inspired, or in any case accelerated, countermeasures by the Latins. And one may perhaps assume that the American Protestants' witness, however implicit, to the desirability and viability of the separation between Church and State did not escape the notice of certain Syrian Christians.

The Protestant influence, though hardly the dominant one, can be seen in the great al-Bustānī (himself a Maronite-turned-Protestant); not merely in the range of his learning and curiosity but in the idea, which he was first to articulate, of a Syria embracing with equal sympathy her sundry confessions and constructed on the basis of a historic Arabic culture wedded to Western thought and institutions. The problem which was of course to plague the Muslim was the desirability, even when one assumed the possibility, of separating his heritage into distinct Islamic and Arabic components.

At all events the Protestant evangelical impulse became subordinate in the course of the nineteenth century to the educational one. The Syrian Protestant College and the Latins' reply to it, the Université Saint-Joseph, took their places as the two major academic establishments in Syria and her main centers of Christian cultural activity. Yet neither the cultural nor the political effects of each institution were to be altogether analogous; and the differences derived at once from the political interests of the French as opposed to the political disinterestedness of the Americans in Syria, and from the history and aspirations of Uniates (particularly the Maronites) on one hand and non-Uniates on the other. For the French-Jesuit university not unnaturally held greatest attraction for Maronites and other Uniates, while the Orthodox Melkites and other non-Uniates, in the absence of their own institutions of higher learning, felt the attractive force of the Protestant progenitor of the American University of Beirut.

But if education at Saint-Joseph tended to leave one with a sense of French cultural and political omnipotence and to foster Lebanese and, to a much lesser extent, Syrian identity, it served to crystallize only those tendencies which had been long operative among the Maronite and in some degree the Uniate Melkite populations of the Lebanon, and which in the nineteenth century had become even more pronounced. The Lebanon had emerged after 1860 as a distinct political unit whose semiautonomy under a Christian governor was recognized by the Ottoman authority. The power of the Druze aristocracy had been destroyed, though only at the cost of thousands of Maronite lives, and the Maronites were politically and numerically preponderant. The Mountain was the only region in Syria where, in the aftermath of the Egyptian occupation, Ottoman centralization had failed to carry the day. Historically the mountaineers had never yielded willingly their autonomy to the government of the low-lying areas of Syria. Now—dominant in their ramparts as never before, ever fearful of submergence in a Syrian or Arab Muslim sea, beckoned by the light emanating from Rome and Paris, and actively encouraged by French missionaries and consuls—the Maronites were to become wholeheartedly committed to Lebanese particularism.[97] This is not to say that yearnings wide enough to include the rest of Syria, with which they shared so much in common, were entirely missing. Nor were they unaffected by French imperial ambitions which *were* wide enough to embrace the whole of Syria. But for those few Maronite writers who toyed with the Greater Syria idea (even within the context of a decentralized Ottoman Empire)

[97] A pre-World War I statement of this position is contained in M. Jouplain (Būluṣ Nujaym), *La Question du Liban* (Paris, 1908), pp. vii, 574, 576-77, 583, 587, 589-90.

the key word with reference to the Lebanon was always "federation."[98]

For the Uniate Melkites too the notion of an autonomous Lebanon (and after World War I an independent Lebanon) was not without its appeal, particularly for those of them living in the Mountain. And while those outside the Lebanon—and these were in the majority—were not averse to the creation of a distinct Lebanese political unit, presided over by Maronites and tied in some way to France, they could scarcely view it with the same enthusiasm which gripped the Maronites. The Uniate Melkites in the last quarter of the nineteenth century were, moreover, already half enveloped by that cultural ambivalence which still tends to characterize them. Their long and extreme dependence on the European connection for education, commercial privilege, and diplomatic protection, and their only partially successful struggle to reconcile the conflicting claims of their Eastern and Western ecclesiastical affinities were unmitigated, in contrast to the case of the Maronites, by possession of a distinct geographical unit in which they could resolve the question of their own identity. No less significant was the fact that their lay leadership derived from an enormously prosperous bourgeoisie which by turn of century was concentrated in Egypt and sufficiently Levantinized to frown upon the study of Arabic.

The Uniate Melkite luminaries who dotted the nineteenth-century cultural scene—the poets and philologists Nāṣīf and Ibrāhīm al-Yāzijī; the Taqlā brothers who

[98] See the remarks of the Maronite, Chekri Ganem (Shukrī Ghānim), in his preface to Georges Samné, *La Syrie* (Paris, 1920), p. xviii.

founded in Cairo in 1875 the newspaper *Al-Ahrām*; Shiblī Shumayyil, physician, agnostic, passionate Darwinian, and science popularizer; and Fransīs Marrāsh, physician, traveler, secularist, and would-be educational reformer—were to have few counterparts in the first half of the twentieth century. True culture-carriers and possessing a political vision that extended beyond that of a Western-oriented Lebanon they were not, however, products of the nineteenth-century Melkite mainstream. With the exception of Marrāsh, none hailed from the cosmopolitan urban centers in Syria and Egypt, or from the large towns of the Lebanon, where the Uniate Melkites and their Latin mentors could be found in strength. It is surely relevant that the al-Yāzijīs, the Taqlās and Shumayyil all hailed from the same Lebanese village;[99] that Shumayyil was one of the very few Uniates who braved the medical school of the Syrian Protestant College and of course emerged not unmarked; and that the al-Yāzijīs and Taqlās are clans which boasted then as now an Orthodox Melkite preponderance. (It will be recalled that the first of the Uniate al-Yāzijīs, 'Abdallāh, had embraced Rome virtually out of necessity.[100]) These men had undergone their formative period in an environment relatively free of Latin missionaries and the Franco-papal orientation which so effectively enveloped the Uniate Melkite bourgeoisie and, to some extent as well, those rural elements located in traditionally Uniate (Maronite) country. In most essentials, indeed, they bore greater resemblance to their Orthodox neighbors and kinsmen than to the Uniate Melkite élite. Nāṣīf al-Yāzijī knew no language

[99] Kafrshīmā, not far from Beirut.
[100] *Above*, p. 67 & n. 90.

save Arabic. The Aleppine, Marrāsh, for his part, had for sire a man who had authored a vigorous defense of the Orthodox position on the *filioque*.[101]

The Uniate Melkites were rare who, in the first quarter of this century, managed to speak with a political and cultural relevance which extended beyond the area of specifically Uniate interests. The Muṭrān family of Ba'albak, Zaḥlah, and Egypt, and the singular Najīb 'Āzūrī, may be counted among the few. But even among the Muṭrāns the political vision tended to narrow progressively to the confines of the Lebanon, the area of greatest Uniate-French influence. It is to be remembered that one of them was sentenced to life imprisonment during the First World War for having enlisted the support of the French consul in a scheme which, at war's end, would have sought the annexation of the Biqā' and Ba'albak to an independent Lebanon.[102]

As to the *sui generis* Najīb 'Āzūrī (d. 1916), while his advocacy of an Arab Empire caressed at its extremities by the Tigris-Euphrates, the Isthmus of Suez, the Mediterranean and the Gulf of Oman, and presided over by

[101] L. Shaykhū, *Al-Ādāb al-'Arabīyah fī al-Qarn al-Tāsi' Ashar*, Vol. II (2 vols.; Beirut, 1924-26), pp. 40-41; Graf, III, 164.

[102] G. Antonius, *The Arab Awakening* (New York, 1946), pp. 185-86; P. Rondot, *Les Chrétiens d'Orient* (Paris, 1955), pp. 121-22. In a book written at the start of World War I, Nadrah Muṭrān wrote: "But if it is indispensable to submit all the parties of Syria to a common authority, to the same laws, it is also opportune to accord, to each province, a certain decentralization, appropriate to satisfy its self-respect or its justifiable liberties" (N. Moutran, *La Syrie de Demain* [4th ed.; Paris, 1916], p. 220). And shortly after the War's end, the Uniate Melkite, Georges Samné, insisted that "Lebanon must be allowed to incorporate herself into the Syrian confederation without losing any of her rights or privileges" (Samné, p. 232).

"the constitutional and liberal monarchy of an Arab sultan,"[103] could only have made his cosectaries blanch, it was an authentically Uniate (and/or French-subsidized) voice which managed simultaneously to uphold the autonomy of the Lebanon, to laud the French occupation of Algeria and to phrase such panegyrics to France as:

> Of all European powers, France is the one which offers, to the oppressed and unfortunate, the most generous and most spontaneous assistance. . . . For several centuries, she has protected the missionaries and the Catholics of the East, without seeking to obtain advantage from this protection. . . . Protectress of the oppressed, France is also one of the brightest torches of civilization and liberty. . . ,[104]

and more ominously:

> Of all the powers which nourish claims upon Syria, France is the one which possesses there the most interests, influence, sympathy and incontestable historic rights. . . .[105]

Nor can one ignore the fact that 'Āzūrī grounds his criticisms of the papacy not only in his nationalist's aversion to Rome's insistence on maintaining the distinctions in rite and ecclesiastical discipline which separated one Uniate Church from another—in 'Āzūrī's view a policy at once fatuous and disruptive of national unity[106]—but in his Francophile's conviction that Rome ought recognize

[103] Negib Azoury, *Le Réveil de la Nation Arabe* (Paris [1905], p. 1).

[104] *Ibid.*, pp. 101-102.

[105] *Ibid.*, p. 94.

[106] *Ibid.*, pp. 167-69.

Her Eldest Daughter as sole protectress of the Uniates and the Latin missionaries.[107]

## XI

The nineteenth century saw forces at play among the Orthodox Melkites which were to transform the community from victim to actor. The revival of the ports of Beirut and Tripoli, and the internal security ushered in by the Egyptian occupation and continued after the Ottoman reentry, brought to the sizable Orthodox populations of the cities of the coast and interior an unprecedented prosperity. Through this development the community which, in the aftermath of the Melkite schism, seemed in danger of reduction to a preserve of peasants and petty artisans had restored to it a vigorous, wealthy and aware bourgeois leadership. These and more humble Orthodox availed themselves of the few primary and secondary schools established by their community, especially after mid-century, as well as the educational facilities provided by the Latins, Protestants, and, later in the century, the Russians.

Higher education meant, of course, the Jesuit university or the Syrian Protestant College. For obvious reasons the Orthodox found the latter somewhat more congenial though, for the vast majority who managed to retain, however nominally, their faith, total identification with either institution and, more importantly, with the Western culture which had spawned them was impossible. More than any other numerically significant Christian community in Syria, the Orthodox were evolving as a

[107] *Ibid.*, pp. 116, 120-21.

community, responsive to Western influences but firmly rooted in the context of geographic Syria, sharing little of the Maronites' commitment to Lebanese particularism or their, and especially the Uniate Melkites', cultural alienation. The attitude of the Orthodox toward the West, however worshipful at times, was always conditioned by an awareness of having been victims, as well as beneficiaries, of Western penetration. In a word, they could never quite forget that the Latin and Protestant missionary assaults had been directed primarily against them and that the early carriers of European civilization (and this was especially true of the Protestants) had seen their history and ecclesiastical traditions as essentially perverse. Whether impelled by doctrinal conviction or thwarted evangelical impulse, the Reverend Henry H. Jessup, D.D. spoke the sentiments of two generations of Presbyterian toilers in the Syrian vineyard when, in the last decade of the nineteenth century, he advised:

> In the year 1819 the first American missionaries came to Western Asia, bringing the Gospel of Christ to the Mohammedans, but in their explorations they came in contact with these various Oriental Christian sects. They found them to be ignorant, illiterate, superstitious, idolatrous. . . . It is a painful and sickening spectacle to enter a Greek church and see the crowds of worshippers burning incense, lighting tapers, and bowing before the filthy, painted boards and then devoutly kissing them and crossing themselves. . . . The Greek Church stands condemned from its own authorized symbols as polytheistic, idolatrous, and unscriptural.[108]

[108] H. H. Jessup, *The Greek Church and Protestant Missions* (New York, 1891), pp. 6, 18, 22.

And yet what was to be a characteristic Orthodox response had been phrased almost a half century earlier by the remarkable As'ad Khayyāṭ, a man sympathetic to certain features of Protestantism and to nineteenth-century European civilization in general; but a man who personified the dilemma confronting those Orthodox Melkites attracted by the West but caught between the ambitions of their Protestant and Latin mentors. As a youth eager for mastery of Italian, Khayyāṭ had been tutored by a Capuchin in Beirut until his parents sensed the friar's failure perfectly to distinguish between linguistic and religious instruction.[109] From the Protestant missionaries he was to receive apparently more disinterested instruction, as well as certain material assistance, but these only in combination with the Protestants' abiding contempt for Khayyāṭ's religious tradition. ". . . God," admonished Khayyāṭ in a voice charged with pride and no little defensiveness,

> has not left himself without witnesses in Asia among the descendents of the primitive Christians. . . . The existence of these Oriental Christians is a stupendous wonder, exposed as they have been for thousands of years to every kind of death arising from political storms, tyranny, persecution, and ignorance. . . .[110] Certainly, Eastern Christians will listen to no one who tells them they must all perish with their fathers before them, unless they adopt some new system from the West. . . .[111] If there is a wish to benefit Syria, it cannot be effected by causing schisms in the

[109] Kayat, pp. 33-34.
[110] *Ibid.*, pp. 158-59.
[111] *Ibid.*, p. 149.

Melkite Eastern Church of Antioch, but care must rather be taken to do good within that Church.[112]

Khayyāṭ wrote as the concerned believer. Yet his Eastern anchor would be employed by Orthodox Melkites into the present, by secularists of the most nominal faith no less than by believers. Albert Hourani has remarked the "eastern Christian consciousness"[113] of the Orthodox-born Faraḥ Anṭūn (1874-1922), disciple of Renan and avowed secularist. His *was* of course an "eastern Christian consciousness" but the further point must be made that since the mid-eighteenth century this consciousness had come to dwell most perfectly among the non-Uniates, and this the logical consequence of not merely their religious tradition but the abrasive character of their recent contact with the representatives of Western Christianity.

Yet the Syrian-Arab awareness that had been in some evidence among the Orthodox Melkites since the last half of the eighteenth century was quickened in the nineteenth by other than Western missionary hostility. Let it be emphasized once again that the Orthodox population was distributed more widely over Syria than any other sect, Christian or Muslim. But located everywhere, they were everywhere a minority; and the memory of past ecclesiastical dislocations wrought or heightened by political fragmentation was never lost. It was altogether inevitable that the political vision of the Orthodox Melkites would correspond roughly to the territorial extent of the Patriarchate of Antioch and, for many, that of Jerusalem as well. In a word, the political vision tended to embrace geographic Syria.

[112] *Ibid.*, p. 189.
[113] Hourani, *Arabic Thought*, p. 259.

Their growing hostility toward the Greek hierarchy was yet another force shaping the political and cultural consciousness of the Orthodox Melkites. By the mid-nineteenth century the Greek hierarchy had outlived their role as bulwark against further Uniate inroads; and their own sharpened ethnic awareness (particularly after the Greek revolution of 1820) served only to provoke a reaction among Syrians, prepared and anxious to assume ecclesiastical control and already humiliated sufficiently by Latins and Protestants. The rapid displacement of Greek by Syrian prelates followed the election in 1898 of the first Syrian patriarch since 1720. His election itself was the result of three factors: the pressure generated by the Orthodox Melkites themselves, the disinclination of the Ottoman government, after Greek independence and the endemic Greco-Ottoman warfare of the nineteenth century, to uphold a Greek hierarchy; and, finally, the diplomatic pressure of Russia.[114]

Well into the nineteenth century the active interest of Russia in the Orthodox subjects of the Sultan had been confined to the Balkans. The faithful of Syria were, of course, not oblivious to the existence of the one free Orthodox power on earth. Contact between the Russians and the Antiochian hierarchy, moreover, had been maintained throughout the Ottoman period,[115] and, in the first decade

[114] On the patriarchal election of 1898, see Mīkhā'īl Burayk, *Al-Ḥaqā'iq al-Waḍīyah fī Ta'rīkh al-Kanīsah al-Anṭākiyah al-Urthudhuksīyah*, ed. S. Qab'īn (Cairo, 1903), pp. 73ff (these pages are authored by the editor Qab'īn); Azoury, pp. 69-71; Asad Rustum, *Kanīsah Madīnah Allāh Anṭākiyah al-'Uẓmā*, Vol. III (3 vols.; Beirut, 1958-??), pp. 241-76.

[115] Patriarch Joachim ibn Ḍaww traveled to Russia in 1584 (Makāriyūs al-Za'īm, fol. 128; Burayk, *Asāmī*, fol. 122), and

of the nineteenth century, we hear of the expectation of the Orthodox peasantry of southern Syria that the hour approached when "the Yellow King" (*al-malik al-aṣfar*) would take upon himself their and Syria's deliverance from the Muslim yoke.[116] The high hope of these Orthodox peasants notwithstanding, it was only with the separation of most of the Balkan Orthodox from the Ottoman Empire that the Tsar turned toward the Syrian faithful. Initially the Russian effort was focused entirely on Palestine—its Holy Places and its Arabic-speaking population under the Greek-dominated Patriarchate of Jerusalem. But while the more numerous Syrians of the Patriarchate of Antioch went largely unattended by the forces of the Third Rome until the 1860's, between that time and the Bolshevik Revolution Russia succeeded in establishing a network of primary and secondary schools which, while achieving most in Palestine, were not without importance for the rest of Syria.[117]

The effect of the Russian presence which most concerns us was the stimulation it afforded the ethnic and linguistic awareness of the Orthodox Melkites. Partly because they

---

Patriarch Macarius al-Za'īm spent several years there on two different occasions in the 1650's and 1660's (Būlus al-Za'īm, pp. 67ff; M. Spinka, "Patriarch Nikon and the Subjection of the Russian Church to the State," *Readings in Russian History*, ed. S. Harcave [New York, 1962], I, 242). After the Greeks assumed direct control over the see of Antioch in 1724, contact with the Russians, through the ecumenical patriarchate, was of course general.

116 Burckhardt, p. 40. Although Burckhardt refers to these peasants simply as "Christians," their location leaves no doubt that they were Orthodox.

117 See A. L. Tibawi, *British Interests in Palestine, 1800-1901* (Oxford, 1961), pp. 173-77; A. L. Tibawi, *American Interests in Syria, 1800-1901* (Oxford, 1966), pp. 158-59, 225-27, 288-89.

sought elimination of Greek influence and partly because Orthodox tradition prescribes use of the indigenous tongue for liturgical purposes, the Russian primary and secondary schools emphasized, as most of their Latin counterparts never had, the study of Arabic. (Let us pause to observe the dismay of an Arab Protestant pastor in 1877 upon hearing Orthodox students at the Russian college in Nazareth chanting the poems of the great Muslim mystic, 'Umar ibn al-Fāriḍ [d. 1235].)[118] An Orthodox Melkite passing through a Russian school emerged with his Arabic strengthened and his growing Syrian-Arab awareness in no way damaged; indeed no fewer than three members of the fervently nationalistic Syro-American school of writers, including the renowned Mīkhā'īl Nu'aymah, attended the college at Nazareth.[119] But despite the fondness for Mother Russia which even Communism has failed to extract from the breast of the Orthodox Melkites, Russian influence and Russian schools came too late and died too quickly to leave the indelible mark left by the Latin and Protestant institutions. The important point is that the Russians fostered rather than impaired the Syrian-Arab consciousness of their cosectaries. They did not leave the Orthodox Melkites with that cultural and political ambiguity which characterized their Uniate brethren.

[118] Tibawi, *British Interests*, pp. 175-76.

[119] The two others were the Ḥimṣī poet Nasīb 'Arīḍah and his cousin and brother-in-law, the essayist and journalist 'Abd al-Masīḥ Ḥaddād, both of whom lived out their adult lives in New York City. 'Arīḍah and Ḥaddād, like Nu'aymah, were members of *al-Rābiṭah al-Qalamīyah* (The Pen Bond), a group of some dozen men who comprised the core of the Syro-American school. It is to be noted that every member, save Jibrān Khalīl Jibrān, was an Orthodox Melkite by birth and, at least by virtue of nominal affiliation, so remained.

Obviously, however, the Orthodox Melkites availed themselves of the educational opportunities proffered by the Protestant and Catholic schools as well as the Orthodox establishments of the Russians. Now despite the fact that no European institution in Syria in the nineteenth century—not excluding the Syrian Protestant College—could offer much more than a glimpse of the substance and implications of Western culture, it is equally a fact that the attractive power of European civilization has never been wholly the function of one's understanding of it. What could hardly fail to arouse the enthusiasm of the non-Muslims of the Muslim empire were, of course, the apparent bases of the political order of liberal Europe—the territorial, the ethnic, the linguistic, the secular, and the constitutional. *This* was the Europe which fired the imagination of certain Orthodox Melkites and further conditioned them for their unique role in the Syrian and Arab nationalist movements of the twentieth century. Their geography and ecclesiastical history (a prime ingredient being, of course, the nature of the contact with both varieties of Western missionaries) obliged the Orthodox Melkite to view his destiny in Syrian (and later in Arab) terms. Western norms of political and social organization, however imperfectly perceived, seemed to provide keys to defining those terms in a manner acceptable to the Syrian Muslim. For, with whatever reluctance, the Orthodox Melkite, in contrast to the Maronite and to some degree the Uniate Melkite as well, could only conceive of a polity in which the Syrian Muslims would be the numerically dominant element. The unencumbered development of the Orthodox Melkites then depended finally upon the Muslim's abandonment of a polity grounded in Islamic law and institutions. A question never broached was whether the secular society thus implied would in fact favor the fulfillment of the Orthodox Church and community as such, or merely advance the mundane interests of individuals who might claim membership in the Church. Little heed was paid the possibility that the secular sword might slice its way through more than the Islamic conception of the proper relationship between Church and State.

## XII

THE EVENTS of the nineteenth century and the intellectual ferment of the second age of transmission could not leave the Muslim élite untouched. It is in no way an exaggeration to state that during the nineteenth century their every traditional attitude was bruised and, in many instances, damaged perhaps beyond restoration. Acutely aware, particularly after 1875, of Islamic society's overall weakness in face of the West—the sacred law which upheld their dominance undermined by the Egyptian occupation of Syria and by the Ottoman reforms which, largely as a result of Western pressures, followed thereupon; their society's economic vitality undermined by its incapacity to withstand or adjust to the assaults of European industrialization—the Muslims too sought after a new pivot.

They were at once aided and harassed by the proliferation after 1860 of Arabic periodicals and newspapers, published and written for the most part by Syrian Christians in their homeland (particularly Beirut) and after 1882 in the less repressive atmosphere of British Egypt. For these unprecedented publishing ventures brought their readers not only news and popular treatment of Western thought and institutions from many aspects, but bold new usage of Arabic in prose and poetry and, particularly in the writings of an erstwhile student at the Syrian Protestant College, the Orthodox Melkite Jurjī Zaydān (d. 1914), a view of Near Eastern history in which Islam appeared as merely an ingredient—albeit the most important one—of a wider Arabic culture.[120] Yet for the Muslim to reconstruct his shattered world on the basis of Western political and social categories was, of course, far more difficult than anything the Christians (not excepting the Orthodox Melkites) were called upon to do. For the Christian the secular viewpoint represented by Zaydān and others, whatever political form it were to take and however destructive of the Church it might ultimately prove, seemed to promise that equality, that full range of mundane possibility, which had been denied him since the Islamic conquest. For the Muslim, on the other hand, it meant sharing political and cultural hegemony with those he had governed for a millennium. Moreover, any ethnic and linguistic awareness the Arabic-speaking Muslim possessed—and it was not inconsiderable—was bound so thoroughly to Islam as to be virtually indistinguishable from it. Islam, in his view, had given the Arab his glory and the integrating element in his culture. Only by slow degrees and with infinite pain was the secular-nationalist viewpoint which came to be represented by the Christians generally, but in its broadest form by the Orthodox Melkites, to make

[120] This is clearly the tendency of Zaydān's many historical novels as well as his more scholarly ventures (Jurjī Zaydān, *Ta'rīkh Ādāb al-Lughah al-'Arabīyah* [4 vols.; Cairo, 1911-14]; Jurjī Zaydān, *Ta'rīkh al-Tamaddun al-Islāmī* [5 vols.; Cairo, 1902-1907]).

a place for itself in the Muslim mentality. There is more than a touch of irony in the fact that Islamic reaction led certain Arab Muslim apologists toward half-embrace of the Arab nationalist idea.

Understandably enough, the initial response of the Arab Muslim to the Western impact had been less an attempt to understand the secret of Western strength than to shore up the ideological defenses of Islam.[121] And as certain Arab Muslims, notably the Aleppine al-Kawākibī (d. 1903) saw it, one major weakness of the Muslim world was that the Turks were charged with a generous portion of its political destiny. It was the Turk, after all, who had stood motionless as Islam wandered from the reign of reason, from the egalitarianism and individual freedom natural to it, and became mired in the less salutary varieties of innovation (*bid'ah*) and imitation (*taqlīd*). It was the same Turk whose tyranny had served merely to accelerate Muslim decline.[122] Only the still uncorrupted Arabs (or more precisely the Arabs of the Peninsula), the argument ran, the original carriers of Islam, could revive Muslim fortunes. But "corruption" had its various facets and neither al-Kawākibī nor other Arab apologists were entirely untainted. The Aleppine's insistence upon the superiority of Arab to Turk, his concept of a revived Arabian caliphate as an en-

[121] The Tunisian Khayr al-Dīn (1810-89) and the Egyptian al-Ṭahṭāwī (1801-73) would appear to be outstanding exceptions to this generalization. But, as Albert Hourani reminds us, "Tahtawi lived and worked in a happy interlude of history, when the religious tension between Islam and Christendom was being relaxed and had not yet been replaced by the new political tension of east and west" (Hourani, *Arabic Thought*, p. 81).

[122] 'Abd al-Raḥmān al-Kawākibī, *Ṭabā'i' al-Istibdād* (Cairo, n.d.), pp. 24-28, 32-36.

tirely spiritual office,[123] and the propensity of men like Muḥammad 'Abduh and Rashīd Riḍā for "casting Islamic principles in the mold of modern liberalism,"[124] clearly testified to a more and more pronounced tendency on the part of Muslims to view their civilization in terms of Western criteria. Directly and indirectly the work of the Syrian Christians and the second age of transmission had not a little to do with this.

In the first decade of the twentieth century the catchword which lent a semblance of unity to the political aspirations of Syrian Christians and Muslims (excluding of course the pan-Islamist minority) was "decentralization." Predictably it held a different meaning for all involved. For the Syrian Muslim it meant something of an Arab-Turkish dual monarchy in which the Islamic idea, though rarely defined, was nevertheless assumed. In a very basic sense Turco-Arab federation represented an effort—obviously, not always on the conscious level—to preserve some measure of Islamic unity. For most of the Maronites and Uniate Melkites (particularly those living in and near the Mountain) it meant the widest possible autonomy for the Lebanon. For most of the Orthodox Melkites and the small but economically and intellectually important Protestant community (itself carved largely out of the Ortho-

[123] 'Abd al-Raḥmān al-Kawākibī, *Umm al-Qurā* (Aleppo, 1959), especially pp. 217-22.

[124] M. H. Kerr, *Islamic Reform* (Berkeley, 1966), p. 174. Kerr pronounces this judgment against Rashīd Riḍā specifically but it is equally applicable to Muḥammad 'Abduh whose *Al-Islām wa al-Naṣrānīyah* (Cairo, 1954) may be legitimately regarded as largely an effort to refute Christianity in terms of its lack of suitability to the canons of Western liberal thought rather than to the principles of traditional Islam.

dox and with a similar geographic distribution) it usually implied an entity embracing all of geographic Syria. An appearance of unity among those adhering to such essentially divergent positions was possible only so long as the Ottoman government continued to turn a deaf ear to cries for any sort of decentralization. But even before the First World War destroyed the Empire, the Young Turks' policy of centralization and Turkification had seriously diminished any hope of federation between Arab and Turkish equals and impelled the Syrian Muslim, inexorably if gradually, toward a broadly based Arab nationalism as a last attempt to shore some fragment against the ruin of Islamic universalism.

With the World War, of course, the former advocates of decentralization broke up into their component parts. Predictably the Maronites and other Lebanese Uniates simply turned from any idea of federation to the prospect of independence. The French Mandate was regarded by the great majority of Uniates as a desirable passage toward that end. "*Mais la France est en Syrie*," exulted the Maronite Lebanese nationalist Shukrī Ghānim, "*—on se le répète comme un refrain berceur et consolant*."[125]

The Orthodox Melkite position was not less predictable, though lacking the virtual unanimity which characterized the Uniate position. The Orthodox viewed the establishment of the French Mandate with feelings ranging from enthusiasm on the part of the most Westernized (these a minority of the Lebanese Orthodox) to uneasiness and

[125] See Ghānim's preface to Georges Samné's book (Samné, p. XVII); also Jouplain, pp. 576-77. That Ghānim, among Uniates, did not stand alone is amply demonstrated by H. N. Howard, *The King-Crane Commission* (Beirut, 1963), pp. 124, 126, 135, 149.

even dismay on the part of the majority. And although the Orthodox Melkites provided the only significant Christian support for the Arab state envisaged by the Sharīf of Mecca and his son Fayṣal, there is scarcely any doubt that the most favored political arrangement was one which would have most nearly corresponded to the geographic dispersion of the Arabic-speaking Orthodox, particularly those subject to the Patriarchate of Antioch.[126] Such a political arrangement could only be, of course, some variation on the theme of geographic Syria—and a geographic Syria free of the Mandate of Catholic France.

It may be seriously argued that it was this aspiration, rooted so firmly in the remote and recent history of the Orthodox Melkites, which spawned the Syrian National Party, founded in the 1930's by the Orthodox Anṭūn Sa'ādah and with a largely Orthodox following.[127] Still in existence and occasionally capable of eruption, the Party's failure to date may prove a permanent feature. Sa'ādah and his devoted cadres had, after all, set themselves the formidable task of eliminating, on one flank, the Lebanese particularism of the Maronites and fellow Uniates and, on the other, the unwillingness of the Muslim majority to admit of a polity which denied them all hope for the eventual inclusion of as much Arab territory as possible.

[126] *Ibid.*, pp. 109, 116, 124, 126, 128, 135-36, 149.

[127] The author of a study on the Syrian National Party offers the firm opinion that the appeal of the Party lay more with Christians than with Muslims. His qualifying phrase, "While it may be extremely difficult to prove this point statistically, there is sufficient internal evidence to corroborate it," could with equal justification be used to qualify our hypothesis that the majority of the Party membership was not merely Christian but Orthodox Melkite (see L. Zuwiyya-Yamak, *The Syrian Social Nationalist Party* [Cambridge, Mass., 1966], p. 142).

Even when full allowance is made for the personal motives of the ruler of Syria, Ḥusnī al-Za'īm, the circumstances of Sa'ādah's death remain instructive: extradition from Syria to Lebanon at the instance of the latter, and there executed as a traitor. Few were the Uniates and fewer still the Sunnī Muslims who mourned.

Should one accept the hypothesis that the growing pan-Arab sentiment of the Syrian Muslims was, at bottom, a secular mutation of Islamic universalism it would follow that the interest of the Orthodox Melkites, after the apparent failure of Syrian nationalism, lay in ensuring that the mutation remained secular. For all the historical romanticism surrounding its manifestos, the one political party today which provides something of an ideological basis for a thoroughgoing secular Arab nationalism is the Ba'th. It cannot be merely fortuitous that one of the two founders of the Party and its chief ideologue is the Damascene Orthodox, Michel 'Aflaq.[128]

Driven from Syria by the Party he had created, 'Aflaq, like a minor Trotsky reduced to Mexico, sat an exile in the Lebanon until called by the Iraqi faithful to adorn their rival Ba'thī regime in Baghdad. But the enthusiasm once inspired by the Ba'th, at least among the younger intelligentsia, has been since June 1967 largely diverted to the Palestinian guerrillas, on that host to wax infinitely stronger than any devotion ever favored the Party of the Melkite Damascene. And in contemplating the running sore that is the struggle for Palestine, we might err in at-

[128] As with the Syrian National Party it is virtually impossible to obtain a precise confessional breakdown of Ba'th Party membership. It is altogether likely, however, that a large majority of the Christian membership is in fact Orthodox Melkite.

taching no significance to the fact that the Popular Front for the Liberation of Palestine (of the radical and ideological guerrilla organizations perhaps the most successful) has for guide one George Ḥabash—of stock Palestinian and Orthodox Melkite.[129]

## XIII

It would perhaps be useful to conclude with an analogy which suggests that the parts played by the three major Syrian Christian communities in accelerating and focusing those forces which are yet reshaping the Arab Muslim world are no more accidental than were (are) the parts played by Jews in framing the ideologies and institutional arrangements of "post-Christian" Europe. But it would be permissible to speak generically of Syrian Christians, as of Jews, only with regard to the realization which all held in common, that there was presented finally the opportunity to break the yoke of their marginality, to create an ideology and community sufficiently broad (or, in the case of the Zionist and to a much lesser extent the Lebanese Christian nationalist, sufficiently *narrow*) to encompass them as full and equal participants. For, as we have seen, the roles which the three Syrian Christian communities assumed, or into which they were thrust, differed in aspiration if not in their essential dynamic; and the differences derived logically from the special features of each community's relationship with the West as well as its historic experience within Islamic society.

[129] It is worth noting too that one of the more conspicuous members of the executive committee of the main guerrilla group, the Palestine Liberation Organization, is Kamāl Nāṣir, Orthodox Melkite and former Ba'thī.

The future is by no means certain. The Maronites with their Lebanese particularism would deem themselves ill-served by the triumph of a pan-Arab nationalism which could not discard the tacit assumption that to be perfectly the Arab is to be also a Muslim. So too would the Uniate Melkites—their economic position in Egypt undone, their Western affinities suspect in Syria, and increasing numbers of them drifting physically to the Lebanon and politically to the Maronite solution.

For the Orthodox Melkites, on the other hand, driven of necessity to closer identification with pan-Arab nationalism, the risks inherent may be no less than the rewards. If, as Louis Gardet suggests, the game will turn ultimately upon the capacity of Arab nationalists, Christian as well as Muslim, to create a City "where the temporal remains charged with religious values" and "to participate in the same humanism, itself wholly dependent upon the Arab-Muslim legacy,"[130] then developments in Europe since the dissolution of "Christendom" would seem to offer little room for optimism in contemplating the Near East in the wake of the dissolution of Islamic universalism. A European humanism born of the Christian legacy, while it existed and no doubt still exists, was never the integrative principle in European and Western society. Has there risen in Europe, in fact, any integrative principle which in relative effectiveness even approaches the discarded Christian one?

Beginning in the nineteenth century, European Jews were prominent in attempts to create the new secular faith (as prominent indeed as certain Syrian Christians in fos-

[130] L. Gardet, "Nationalisme arabe et Communauté musulmane," *Colloque sur la Sociologie Musulmane*, p. 275.

tering secular Near Eastern nationalisms and even something that hints of Gardet's Arab-Muslim humanism) and the adhesion of large numbers of Eastern European Jews to Marxism may be viewed in this light. But it is still to be demonstrated that Marxist universalism (or yet the sundry "secular" nationalisms of Europe) has in practice managed to embrace with equal sympathy gentiles and even that minority of Jews fully prepared to sacrifice as much of their Jewishness as the new faith requires. Nor is this apparent failure wholly explained by unadorned reference to a term such as "anti-Semitism." For if it could have been anticipated that Jews would comprise the vanguard of radical movements in Eastern Europe and Weimar Germany (and, for that matter, the United States in the 1960's and beyond), it might equally have been anticipated that the majority element in each instance would concede but grudgingly, if at all, their right to do so. There is perhaps a price exacted from the traditionally marginal even when they successfully impart to a significant section of the broader society their own sense of alienation.[131]

[131] The Jewish affinity for Marxism, not to mention a variety of radical movements past and present, has yet to receive the close study it deserves. Michels, writing on the eve of World War I, presented a brief, idealized but still useful analysis of Jewish involvement in early socialist movements (Robert Michels, *Political Parties*, trans. Eden and Cedar Paul [New York, 1962], pp. 245-51). Burks, while making no claim to historical depth, offers a brief, sober but incomplete analysis of the role of Jews in Eastern European communism (R. V. Burks, *The Dynamics of Communism in Eastern Europe* [Princeton, 1961], pp. 158-70, 189-90). An article by McGrath and another by Schorske do much to explain the ambivalence which tore German-speaking Jewish liberals in the late nineteenth century as the pan-German nationalism many had

It must be admitted at once that the analogy between the Jew in Christendom and the Christian in the "Abode of Islam" is hardly perfect. Obviously, the Christian's integration into Islamic society had been far more thorough than that of the Jew into Christian society. And it is almost certain that the Muslim Ba'thī, or the Muslim adherent of whatever pan-Arab nationalist movement finally carries the day, will, even if unprompted by an Arab-Muslim humanism, prove more forgiving of the Christian background of men such as Michel 'Aflaq and George Ḥabash than were (are) gentile Marxists (not to mention assorted nationalists—communist and other) of the Jewish origins of some of their most distinguished shapers—men whose right to redefine the order which named them marginal was not granted by the historically dominant community even as it accepted much of their redefinition. Yet it is well to remark the immemorial pressures upon the new order, whatever its formal ideo-

espoused turned away from them (William J. McGrath, "Student Radicalism in Vienna," *Journal of Contemporary History*, 2 [July 1967], 183-201; Carl E. Schorske, "Politics in a New Key: An Austrian Triptych," *The Journal of Modern History*, 39 [December 1967], 365-86); Schorske's treatment of Herzl is particularly noteworthy. The article by Liebman breaks fresh ground and could be profitably supplemented by van den Haag's nontheoretical, rather idealized but informative study of the Jewish ethos (Charles Liebman, "Toward a Theory of Jewish Liberalism," in Donald R. R. Cutler [ed.], *The Religious Situation, 1969* [Boston, 1969], pp. 1034-62; Ernest van den Haag, *The Jewish Mystique* [New York, 1969]). Laqueur's recent comments in *Encounter* may at last inspire serious analysis of the Jewish radical in Weimar Germany (Walter Laqueur, "The Tucholsky Complaint," *Encounter* [October 1969], pp. 76-80). Stanley Rothman's soon-to-be published article, "Portrait of the Jew as Radical," is an unsentimental guide to the direction that future research on this subject might take.

logical statement, to resolve itself as a recognizable variant of the old. Both for the community which has traditionally defined marginality and, it is too often forgotten, for those who have carried its mark the old categories, the old burdens of history are more easily denied than effectively discarded.

# BIBLIOGRAPHY

## OF MATERIAL CITED

### Unpublished: Archives and Manuscripts

L'Archivio della S. Congregazione di Propaganda Fide.

*Congregazioni Particolari.* Vols. 75 (1729), 83 (1745-1746).

*Le Scritture originali riferite nelle Congregazioni Generali.* Vols. 530 (April 14-June 23, 1698), 540 (September 26-December 6, 1701), 598 (March 26-April 8, 1715), 608 (January 25-April 13, 1717), 625 (July 8-August 19, 1720).

*Scritture riferite nei Congressi.* Greci Malchiti Patriarcato Antiocheno e Gerosolomitano. Vols. I (1683-1723), II (1724-1733), III (1734-1738), IV (1739-1744).

Biblioteca Apostolica Vaticana. *Vaticanus Arabicus.*

Mīkhā'īl al-Ḥamawī. Kitāb Farīḍah al-Mawārīth. MS 54.

Makāriyūs al-Za'īm. Asāmī Baṭārikah Anṭākiyah min Buṭrus al-Rasūl wa alladhīnā ma'ahu. MS 689.

(Untitled manuscript containing an Arabic translation of the *ekthesis* produced by the Synod of Constantinople, 1722.) MS 161.

Bibliothèque Orientale de Beyrouth. Mīkhā'īl Burayk. Asāmī al-Baṭārikah fī Anṭākiyah min 'Ahd Buṭrus al-Rasūl ilā al-Ān. MS 14.

France. Archives Nationales. *Ministère des Affaires Étrangères.* Correspondance Consulaire.

$B^1$76 (Alep I, 1630-1707),

$B^1$77 (Alep II, 1708-1715),
$B^1$78 (Alep III, 1716-1719),
$B^1$80 (Alep V, 1724-1728),
$B^1$81 (Alep VI, 1729-1732),
$B^1$83 (Alep VIII, 1737-1742),
$B^1$84 (Alep IX, 1743-1745),
$B^1$87 (Alep XII, 1754-1757),
$B^1$401 (Constantinople XXVI, January-June 1730),
$B^1$405 (Constantinople XXX, January-June 1732),
$B^1$1017 (Seyde I, 1645-1704),
$B^1$1018 (Seyde II, 1705-1711),
$B^1$1019 (Seyde III, 1712-1715),
$B^1$1020 (Seyde IV, 1716-1718),
$B^1$1021 (Seyde V, 1719-1725),
$B^1$1022 (Seyde VI, 1726-1730),
$B^1$1023 (Seyde VII, 1731-1735),
$B^1$1024 (Seyde VIII, 1736-1739),
$B^1$1026 (Seyde X, 1742-1745),
$B^1$1033 (Seyde XVII, 1763-1767),
$B^1$1036 (Seyde XX, 1773-1774),
$B^1$1114 (Tripoli de Syrie I, 1667-1715),
$B^1$1115 (Tripoli de Syrie II, 1716-1724),
$B^1$1116 (Tripoli de Syrie III, 1725-1731).

Great Britain. Public Record Office. *State Papers.* 97/20 (Turkey, March 1684-December 1697).

## Published Documents, Chronicles, Memoirs and Travel Accounts

Abel, L. *Une mission religieuse en Orient au xvi$^{e}$ siècle: Relation adressée à Sixte-Quint par l'évêque de Sidon.* Translated by A. d'Avril. Paris, 1866.

Arvieux, Laurent d'. *Mémoires du Chevalier d'Arvieux.* 6 vols. Paris, 1735.

Besson, Joseph. *La Syrie et la terre sainte au XVII$^{e}$ siècle.* Paris, 1862.

Burayk, Mīkhā'īl. *Al-Ḥaqā'iq al-Waḍīyah fī Ta'rīkh al-Kanīsah al-Anṭākiyah al-Urthudhuksīyah*. Edited by S. Qab'īn. Cairo, 1903.

———. *Ta'rīkh al-Shām, 1720-1782*. Edited by Q. al-Bāshā. Ḥarīṣā (Lebanon), 1930.

Burckhardt, J. L. *Travels in Syria and the Holy Land*. London, 1822.

al-Duwayhī, Isṭifānūs. *Ta'rīkh al-Azminah*. Beirut, 1951.

Karāmah, Rūfā'īl. *Maṣādir Ta'rīkhīyah li Ḥawādith Lubnān wa Sūrīyā*. Edited by B. Qaṭṭān. Beirut, 1929.

Kayat, Assaad Y. *A Voice from the Lebanon*. London, 1847.

*Lettres édifiantes et curieuses écrites des missions étrangères*. 5 vols. Toulouse, 1810.

Noradounghian, Gabriel. *Recueil d'actes internationaux de l'empire ottoman*. 3 vols. Paris, 1897-1902.

Rabbath, A. (ed.). *Documents inédits pour servir à l'histoire du christianisme en orient*. 2 vols. Paris, 1905-1907, 1910-1921.

al-Ṣabbāgh, Mīkhā'īl. *Ta'rīkh al-Shaykh Ẓāhir al-'Umar al-Zaydānī*. Edited by Q. al-Bāshā. Ḥarīṣā (Lebanon), n.d.

al-Shidyāq, Ṭannūs. *Kitāb Akhbār al-A'yān fī Jabal Lubnān*. Beirut, 1859.

al-Shihābī, Ḥaydar. *Al-Ghurar al-Ḥisān fī Akhbār Abnā' al-Zamān*. Edited by A. Rustum and F. A. Bustānī. Beirut, 1933.

Volney, C. F. *Voyage en Égypte et en Syrie, 1783-5*. 2 vols. 2d. ed. Paris, 1825.

al-Za'īm, Būlus. *Nukhbah Safrah al-Baṭrīrk Makāriyūs al-Ḥalabī bi Qalam Waladihi al-Shammās Būlus*. Edited by Q. al-Bāshā. Ḥarīṣā (Lebanon), 1912.

### GENERAL

'Abduh, Muḥammad. *Al-Islām wa al-Naṣrānīyah*. Cairo, 1954.

Antonius, G. *The Arab Awakening*. New York, 1946.

Azoury, Negib. *Le Réveil de la Nation Arabe*. Paris [1905].
al-Bāshā, Qusṭanṭīn. *Muḥāḍarah fī Ta'rīkh Ṭā'ifah al-Rūm al-Kāthūlīk fī Miṣr*. Ḥarīṣā (Lebanon), n.d.
Burks, R. V. *The Dynamics of Communism in Eastern Europe*. Princeton, 1961.
Carali, Paul (Qara'lī, Būluṣ). *Les Syriens en Égypte*. Vol. 1: *Au Temps des Mamlouks*. Égypte, n.d. In Arabic.
Gibb, H.A.R. and Bowen, H. *Islamic Society and the West*. Vol. 1: *Islamic Society in the Eighteenth Century*. 2 parts. London, 1950, 1957.
Graf, G. *Geschichte der Christlichen Arabischen Literatur*. 4 vols. and index. Vatican City, 1944-1953.
Hajjar, J. *Les chrétiens uniates du Proche-Orient*. Paris, 1962.
Harik, I. F. *Politics and Change in a Traditional Society: Lebanon, 1711-1845*. Princeton, 1968.
Hitti, P. K. *History of the Arabs*. 8th ed. New York, 1963.
Hourani, A. *A Vision of History*. Beirut, 1961.
———. *Arabic Thought in the Liberal Age*. Oxford, 1967.
Howard, H. N. *The King-Crane Commission*. Beirut, 1963.
Jessup, H. H. *The Greek Church and Protestant Missions*. New York, 1891.
S. Joannes Damascenus. *De Haeresibus Liber*. In Vol. 47 of *Patrologiae Cursus Completus* (Series graeca). Edited by J.-P. Migne. 81 vols. Paris, 1856-1867.
Jouplain, M. (Nujaym, Būluṣ). *La Question du Liban*. Paris, 1908.
al-Kawākibī, 'Abd al-Raḥmān. *Ṭabā'i' al-Istibdād*. Cairo, n.d.
———. *Umm al-Qurā*. Aleppo, 1959.
Kerr, M. H. *Islamic Reform*. Berkeley, 1966.
Michels, Robert. *Political Parties*. Translated by Eden and Cedar Paul. New York, 1962.
Moutran, N. *La Syrie de Demain*. 4th ed. Paris, 1916.
Neale, J. M. *A History of the Holy Eastern Church: The Patriarchate of Antioch*. London, 1873.

Polk, W. R. *The Opening of South Lebanon, 1788-1840*. Cambridge, Mass., 1963.
Rondot, P. *Les Chrétiens d'Orient*. Paris, 1955.
Rustum, Asad. *Kanīsah Madīnah Allāh Anṭākiyah al-'Uẓmā*. 3 vols. Beirut, 1958-?
Salibi, K. S. *The Modern History of Lebanon*. London, 1965.
Samné, Georges. *La Syrie*. Paris, 1920.
Shaykhū, L. *Al-Ādāb al-'Arabīyah fī al-Qarn al-Tāsi' 'Ashar*. 2 vols. Beirut, 1924-1926.
Tibawi, A. L. *American Interests in Syria, 1800-1901*. Oxford, 1966.
——. *British Interests in Palestine, 1800-1901*. Oxford, 1961.
van den Haag, Ernest. *The Jewish Mystique*. New York, 1969.
Zaydān, Jurjī. *Ta'rīkh Ādāb al-Lughah al-'Arabīyah*. 4 vols. Cairo, 1911-1914.
——. *Ta'rīkh al Tamaddun al-Islāmī*. 5 vols. Cairo, 1902-1907.
Zuwiyya-Yamak, L. *The Syrian Social Nationalist Party*. Cambridge, Mass., 1966.

## Articles

Bacel, P. "Nicholas Saïgh, religieux chouérite, 1692-1756," *Echos d'Orient*, XI (March 1908), 71-76.
Bowman, R. A. "Syriac Language and Literature," *Encyclopedia Americana*, 26 (1968 edition), 193-97.
Charon, C. "Silsilah Asāqifah al-Malikīyīn fī Qārā wa Yabrūd wa Tadmur wa Zaḥlah wa al-Zabadānī," *Al-Machriq*, XIII (1910), 328-37.
——. "Silsilah Maṭārinah Kursī Ḥalab," *Al-Machriq*, XI (1908), 536-45.
——. "Silsilah Maṭārinah Kursī Ṣūr," *Al-Machriq*, IX (1906), 412-16.
Gardet, L. "Nationalisme arabe et Communauté musulmane,"

*Correspondance d'Orient, No. 5: Colloque sur la Sociologie Musulmane, actes, 11-14 Septembre 1961* (Bruxelles, 1961?), pp. 265-81.

Karalevskij, C. "Antioche," *Dictionnaire d'Histoire et de Géographie Ecclésiastiques*, III, cols. 563-703.

Laqueur, Walter. "The Tucholsky Complaint," *Encounter* (October 1969), pp. 76-80.

Leibman, Charles. "Toward a Theory of Jewish Liberalism," *The Religious Situation, 1969*, edited by Donald R. R. Cutler (Boston, 1969), pp. 1034-62.

McGrath, William J. "Student Radicalism in Vienna," *Journal of Contemporary History*, 2 (July 1967), 183-201.

Nasrallah, J. "Chronologie des Patriarches d'Antioche de 1500 à 1634," *Proche-Orient Chrétien*, VI (1956), 294-311, VII (1957), 26-43, 207-17, 291-304.

———. "Euthyme II Karmé (Karma)," *Dictionnaire d'Histoire et de Géographie Ecclésiastiques*, XVI, cols. 54-57.

Rothman, Stanley. "Portrait of the Jew as Radical" (forthcoming).

Schacht, Joseph. "Pre-Islamic Background and Early Development of Jurisprudence," *Law in the Middle East*, I, edited by M. Khadduri and H. Liebesny (Washington, D.C., 1955), 28-56.

Shaykhū, L. "Mīkhā'īl al-Ṣabbāgh wa Usratuhu," *Al-Machriq*, VIII (1905), 24-34.

———. "Tarjamah al-Ṭayyib al-Athar al-Khūrī Nīqūlāwus al-Ṣā'igh," *Al-Machriq*, VI (1903), 97-111.

Shaykhū, L. and Charon, C. "Usqufīyah al-Rūm al-Kātūlīk fī Bayrūt," *Al-Machriq*, VIII (1905), 193-204.

Schorske, Carl E. "Politics in a New Key: An Austrian Triptych," *The Journal of Modern History*, 39 (December 1967), 343-86.

Spinka, M. "Patriarch Nikon and the Subjection of the Russian

Church to the State," *Readings in Russian History*, I, edited by S. Harcave (New York, 1962), 229-44.

Tibawi, A. L. "The American Missionaries in Beirut and Butrus al-Bustani," *St. Antony's Papers, Number 16, Middle Eastern Affairs* (London, 1963), pp. 137-82.

Walzer, R. "The Achievement of the Falasifa and their Eventual Failure," *Correspondance d'Orient, No. 5: Colloque sur la Sociologie Musulmane, actes, 11-14 Septembre 1961* (Bruxelles, 1961?), pp. 347-59.

Zayat, H. et Edelby, N. "Les sièges épiscopaux du patriarcat melkite d'Antioche en 1658 d'après un document inédit du Patriarche Macaire III Za'im," *Proche-Orient Chrétien*, III (1953), 340-50.

# INDEX

kite-Maronite union, 23. *See also* Antioch (Melkite Patriarchate of)
Constantinople, Synod of (1722), 48n
consuls, *see* England, France, Latin missions, Maronites, Melkite (Uniates)
Copts, 9
corsairs, 41, 42n, 43, 44n, 45, 47n
Counter-Reformation, 17
Crusaders, 10, 14-15, 23; corsairs as, 41
Crusades, 7, 9, 22
Cyril al-Ṭānās, Melkite Uniate Patriarch (1724-1760), 55 & n, 56 & n, 57n, 76
Cyril al-Za'īm, Melkite Patriarch (1672-1720), 27n, 29n, 45, 47 & n

al-Dabbās, Athanasius, *see* Athanasius al-Dabbās
Damascus, governors (*wālīs*) of, 27 & n, 64 & n, 66 & n; Latin missionaries in, 19n, 47n; legal emancipation of Christians in, 69 & n;
*Melkites of*, bourgeoisie, 47 & n, 50; flight of patriarch, 27n; Orthodox, 29n, 67; traders, 40; Uniates, 47n, 48n, 53, 55, 64 & n, 66; emigration of Uniates, 60;
nature of Ottoman authority in, 29; patriarchal residence in, 29n
Damietta, 40, 41n
Daniel the Chiot, Melkite Patriarch (1767-1792), 66n
Ḍaww, Joachim ibn, *see* Joachim ibn Ḍaww
Dayr al-Qamr, 60
*Demandatam*, 57n
Desalleurs, Pierre, 33n
*dhimmī*, 36, 38, 64n, 67
dragoman, 32, 33n, 36, 39n; honorary, 33 & n, 34, 36, 37n; second, 33n
Druzes, 37, 53, 58-59, 74, *see also* *amīrs*, Lebanon
al-Duwayhī, Isṭifānūs, 62

Ecchellensis, Abraham (al-Haqilānī, Ibrāhīm), 18
ecumenical patriarchate, *see* Constantinople (Patriarchate of)
education, *see* Latin missions, Maronites, Melkites (Orthodox), Melkites (Uniate), Protestants, Russia
Egypt, 7; Copts of, 9; Melkite Uniates in, 40, 50, 51n, 62, 64, 66, 75-77, 95; publications by Syrian Christians in, 87
*ekthesis* of Synod of Constantinople (1722), 49n
Eliano, Jean-Baptiste, 17n
England, consuls in Aleppo, 37n; influence in Ottoman Empire, 39; religious motivation of, 33n, 38; traders of, 34n, 36n, 46, 53
Europe, cultural influence upon Muslims, *see* France, Islam; cultural influence upon Syrian Christians, 3, 5-6, 19 & n, 23, 32, 48, 51-54, 57, 70, 73, 79-82, 86-88, 94, *see also* Maronites, Melkites (Orthodox), Melkites (Uniate) Syrian Christians; humanism, 95; industrialization, 87; merchants and trade in Syria, 32, 69, *see also* England, France; missionaries, 69, *see also* Latin missions, Protestants; powers, 46; protection of Syrian Christians, *see* Maronites, Melkites (Orthodox), Melkites (Uniate); relations with Ottoman Empire, 6, 29-30, 32, 37,

39, 48, 51, 70, 88-90, *see also* Islam Ottoman Empire; travelers, 69
Euthymius the Chiot, Melkite Patriarch (1635-1647), 68n
Euthymius al-Karmah, Melkite Patriarch (1634-1635), 22n
Euthymius al-Ṣayfī, Melkite Uniate Metropolitan of Sidon (1683-1723), as founder of Salvatorians, 55; grasp of classical Arabic, 17n; as Latinizer, 55 & n; letter to Louis XIV, 56; loyalty of Melkites of Sidon to, 47n; problem of corsairs and, 42n, 45 & n

Fakhr al-Dīn al-Ma'nī, 27, 61
Farḥāt, Germanos, 52 & n
*fatwā*, 31 n
*Fayṣal* ibn Ḥusayn, 92
*fermān*, 49n
*filioque*, 77
Florence, Council of, 24
France, ambassadors, 30n, 37; ambassadorial patents, 32 & n; *consuls*, in Acre, *see* Acre; in Aleppo, *see* Aleppo; in Beirut, 58; in Sidon, *see* Sidon; in Tripoli, 33n; factories, 19n, 20n, 33n, 36 & nn, 38-39, 46, 58n, *see also* Acre, Aleppo, Sidon, Tripoli; influence in Ottoman Empire, 30 & n, 31, 37, 39-40; Mandate in Syria, 91-92; merchants and trade in Syria, 34n, 39, 43 & n, 44n, 53; naturalization of Syrian Christians, 32 & n; protection of Maronites, *see* Maronites; protection of Melkite Uniates, *see* Melkites (Uniate); protection of missionaries, *see* Latin missionaries; political ambitions in Syria, 73-74, 78; Royal patents, 32 & n, 33n
Franciscans, 18n, 44n, 53, *see also* Latin missions
Franks, 56
French language, 19

Ganem, Chekri, *see* Ghānim, Shukrī
Gardet, Louis, 95-96
Ghānim, Shukrī (Ganem, Chekri), 75n, 91 & n
al-Ghazzālī, 12
Grand Seigneur, *see* Ottoman Empire
Great Church, *see* Constantinople (Patriarchate of)
Great schism, 23
Greater Syria, 74, *see also* Syria
Greece (ancient), 7
Greek, ecclesiastical literature, 15 & n, 22; learning, 3, 12, *see also* Hellenistic thought; literary culture, 16 & n, 20; liturgy, 16n, 20; speakers in Baghdad, 16n; translations from, 12, 15n, 16n, 52. *See also* Antioch (Melkite Patriarchate of), Constantinople (Patriarchate of)
Greek College in Rome, 18
Greek Revolution, 83
Gregory XIII, Pope, 18

Ḥabash, George, 94, 97
Ḥaddād, 'Abd al-Masīh, 85n
Ḥakīm, Maximos, 56n
al-Ḥamawī, Michael V, see Michael al-Ḥamawī
Hapsburgs, 30, 39, 69
al-Haqilānī, Ibrāhīm, *see* Ecchellensis, Abraham
Ḥarfūsh, house of, 27n
Ḥarrān, 16n
Hellenistic thought, 11, 13, 70, *see also* Greek
Herzl, Theodore, 97n
Ḥimṣ, 66, 85n

Holy Land, 18n, *see also* Palestine
Holy Places, 84
Hourani, Albert, 82, 89n

ibn Ḍaww, Joachim, *see* Joachim ibn Ḍaww
ibn al-Fāriḍ, ʿUmar, 85
ibn Jubayr, Isḥāq, 20n
Ibrāhīm Pasha (of Egypt), 69n
Ibrāhīm Pasha (of Sidon), 36n
Ignatius ʿAṭīyah, Melkite Patriarch (1619-1634), 25n, 27n
Ignatius Peter, 25n
Iraq, 14, 93
Islam (Islamic), Abode of, 9, 96; advance across Anatolia, 21; Arab identity and, 73, 88-89, 95; Arabic literary culture of, 15-17, 19-20, 71, 88, *see also* Arabic; Arab nationalism and, 89, 91-93, 95-96; Armenians under, 9; conquest, 8; conversion to, 8-10, 13, 15, 30; Christianity's encounter with, 7, 89n; domination of urban centers by, 20, 28;
*disintegrative phase of*: 3-6, 86-97; role of Syrian Christians during, 3-6, 70, 86-88, 90-97, *see also* Maronites, Melkites (Orthodox), Melkites (Uniate);
*formative phase of*: 3-6, 11-13, 70; role of Syrian Christians during, 3-4, 10-13, 70;
*institutions of*: 3, 5, 10, 12-13, 86-87, 90; law, 8, 12, 26-28, 69 & n, 86-87; mysticism, 12; theocracy, 11-12, 70n, 87;
Ottoman, *see* Ottoman Empire; pan-, 90; secularism and, 88-89, 93; status of Syrian Christians in, 3, 5, 8, 11, 13-14, 17, 23-25, 27-28, 47, 68, 69 & n, 87-88, 94, 96-97, *see also* Mamlūks, Ottoman Empire; struggle against Byzantines, 14;
*Sunni*, 13, 20, 93; position of heterodox Lebanese *amirs* in, 27-28, 58-59;
Syrian Christian attitude toward, 12, 56, 84, 94; Syrian nationalism and, 92-93; Turkish influence upon, 89, *see also* Ottoman Empire; unity of, 90; universalism, 91, 93, 95; Western influence upon, 3-6, 87-89, 90 & n, *see also* France, Syrian Muslims
Istanbul, 44n, 53, *see also* Constantinople
Italian language, 19

Jacobites, conversion to Islam, 9-10; geographic distribution of, 7, 9; influence upon Islam, 12-13; Latin proselytizing among, *see* Latin missions; missionary activity of, 9-10;
*Monophysitism*: 7, 9; Islamic thrust of christology, 10;
Syriac literature of, 15 & n, *see also* Syriac
Jaffa, 51n
Jawhar, Athanasius, *see* Athanasius Jawhar
Jerusalem, Patriarchate of, 82, 84
Jessup, Henry H., 80
Jesuits, adoption of native dress, 48 & n; advantages over non-Uniate clergy, 23; in Aleppo, 18, 19n, 43n, 44n; in Damascus, 19n; establishment of missions in Syria, 17 & n; feud with Franciscans, 53n; schools in Syria, 19 & n, 73-74. *See also* Latin missions
Jews, 36n, 51n, 94-95, 96 & n, 97
Jibrān, Jibrān Khalīl, 85n
*jizyah*, 37nn, *see also kharāj*, poll tax

in administration of, 50, 51 & n; relative intolerance of, 9
al-Manṣūrī, Sulaymān, 31n
Mār Sābā, monastery of, 68n
marginal community (marginality), *see* Jews, Syrian Christians
Maronite College in Rome, 18, 62
Maronites, 6, 73, 76; *amīrs'* protection of, *see amīrs*; ascendancy in silk production, 60; attempted union with Melkites, 23; attitude toward Near Eastern nationalisms, 28; attitude toward pan-Arab nationalism, 95; attitude toward Syrian nationalism, 74, 92-93; as dragomans, 33n, 39n, 40; education of, 18, 19 & n, 20 & n, 52, *see also* Latin missions; European protection of, 30-31, 32 & n, 34-35, 36 & n, 37 & nn, 38, 39 & n, 40 & n, 41, 43 & n, 44 & nn, 45, 58, 75, *see also beret*, dragoman; geographic distribution of, 8, 10, 13, 28, 40n, 50, 59, 66; Latin missionaries' contact with, 18 & n, 19, 24; Lebanese particularism of, 62, 74-75, 80, 90-92, 95; linguistic arabization of, *see* Arabic; migration into south Lebanon, 59; Monothelitism of, 7, 8 & n; papal concordat with, 58; political preponderance in the Lebanon, 58-60, 74; retention of Syriac liturgy, 20; rise of trading class, 32 & n, 33, 34 & n, 35 & n, 36-38, 39 & n, 40 & n, 41, 42 & n, 43 & nn, 44 & nn, 46-47; shaykhly families, 59; submission to Rome, 7, 17, 22; translations by, 22
Marrāsh, Fransīs, 76-77
Marseille, 35n
Marxism, 96-97
Mediterranean, 77
Melkite Church, *see* Antioch (Melkite Patriarchate of), Melkites (Orthodox), Melkites (Uniate)
Melkites (Orthodox), 6, 62; Arab identity of, 4, 54, 65, 68, 82, 84-86, 88, 92, 93 & n, 95; attempted union with Maronites, 23; attitude toward French Mandate, 91; attitude toward Melkite Uniates, 31n, 48, 56; bourgeoisie, 49-50, 79, *see also* Melkites (Uniate); Byzantine influence upon, 10, 15, *see also* Byzantine, Greek; clergy, 21, 24, 26n, 27-28, 45, 48, *see also* Antioch (Melkite Patriarchate of), Melkites (Uniate);
*demography*: diocesan distribution, 20n, 21n, 28n; geographic distribution, 7, 10, 14, 28-29, 40n, 59, 79, 82, *see also* Melkites (Uniate); numerical superiority over Melkite Uniates, 50; proportion in Syrian population, 10 & n, 13 & n, 50; urban concentration of, 7, 10, 20n, 21n, 24, 28-29, 79;
as dragomans, 39n, 40n, *see also beret*, dragoman, Melkites (Uniate); eastern consciousness of, 81-82; education of, 19n, 22, 24, 50, 61, 73, 79, 84-86, 88, *see also* Latin missions, Protestants; effect of Muslim domination upon, 4-5, 8-14, 25-26, 47, *see also* Islam, Mamlūks, Ottoman Empire; European protection of, *see* Melkites (Uniate), Russia; hostility toward Crusaders, 14; Latin proselytizing among, *see* Latin missions; Lebanese identity of, 91; linguistic arabization of, 15 & nn, 16, 20 & n, 21, 22 & n, 85; *see also* Arabic;

Propaganda, *see* Sacred Congregation for the Propagation of the Faith
Protestants, Arab, 73, 85, 90-91; attitude toward Melkite Orthodox, 80-81; education provided by, 72-73, 76, 79, 86, 88; English, 38; influence in Syria, 72-73, 81, 85; printing of Arabic Bible by, 18; proselytizing among Syrian Christians, 72, 80, 81

*Qāḍī*, 29
al-Qissīs, Yūsuf, 50n

al-Rābiṭah al-Qalamīyah, 85n
Renan, Ernest, 82
Riḍā, Rashīd, 90 & n
Rome (ancient), 7
Rome (papal), 14; 'Āzūrī's criticism of, 78; concordat with Maronites, 58; consular protection and submission to, 42; Cyril al-Za'īm's correspondence with, 45; education of Uniate clergy in, 18-19, 57, 60; Greek College in, 18; initiation of missionary effort, 17; interventions in behalf of Uniate merchants, 42n, 43 & n, 44n, 45; Maronite allegiance to, 7, 17, 22, 28; Maronite College in, 18; Maronite dependence upon, 10, 58; opposition to Latinization, 56-57, 72; problem of corsairs, 45; rationale of Syrian Christian submission to, 30, 47; rationale of Unia, 56; rejection of Jawhar's succession, 56; submission of Athanasius al-Dabbās, 43; subsidies to Eastern prelates, 25 & n. *See also* Latin missions, Sacred Congregation for the Propagation of the Faith
Rosetta, 41n
Russia, Bolshevik Revolution, 84; early contact with Melkites, 24, 83 & n; influence of, 83, 85; protection of Melkite Orthodox, 65; schools in Syria, 79, 84-86

Sa'ādah, Anṭūn, 92-93
al-Ṣabbāgh, Ibrāhīm, 50n, 61n, 66
al-Ṣabbāgh, Sim'ān, 50n
al-Ṣabbāgh, Yūsuf, 51n
Sacred Congregation for the Propagation of the Faith, 17n, 25 & n, 32n, 43, 45, 55n, *see also* Latin missions, Rome (papal)
al-Ṣahyūnī, Jibrā'īl, *see* Sionita, Gabriel
al-Ṣā'igh, Niqūlā, 52 & n, 55n, 56n, 60, 61n
Salibi, K. S., 13n
Salvatorian Congregation, 55, *see also* Euthymius al-Ṣayfī, Melkites (Uniate)
Samné, Georges, 77n
al-Ṣayfī, Euthymius, *see* Euthymius al-Ṣayfī
Schacht, Joseph, 12
schism, Great, *see* Great schism; Melkite, *see* Melkite schism
Selīm I, Sultan, 13, 25-26
Seyde, *see* Sidon
Sharīf of Mecca, 92
*shaykh*, 52
*shaykh al-balad*, 51n
al-Shidyāq, Ṭannūs, 62
al-Shihāb, house of, 37, 59-60, *see also amīrs*, Bashīr I
al-Shihābī, Ḥaydar, 62
Shi'ite, 27n
Shumayyil, Shiblī, 76
Shwayrite Congregation, 54, 55n, 56n, 61n, *see also* Melkites (Uniate)
Sidon, French consuls in, 30n, 33n, 34n, 36nn, 38n, 42 & n,

Tsar, 84
Turco-Arab federation, 70, 90
Turkification, 91
Turkomen, 9
Turks, 43, 44n, 68, 89-90; Young, 91. *See also* Islam, Ottoman Empire

Umayyad Caliphate, 11
Umayyad dynasty, 12
Unia, Uniates, *see* Maronites, Melkites (Uniate), Syrian Christians
Université Saint-Joseph, 73-74
Urban VIII, Pope, 18n

Vatican, 18, 22, *see also* Rome (papal)
Venetians, 53
Versailles, 42
Visir, *see wazīr*

*wālī*, 27n, 29, 30n, 36nn
*wazīr*, 30n, 50n, 61n
Weimar Germany, 96
West, Western, westernization, *see* Europe, France, Islam Lebanon, Maronites, Melkites (Orthodox), Melkites (Uniate)
World War I, 11, 77, 91

al-Yāzijī, 'Abdallāh, 66 & n, 67 & n, 76
al-Yāzijī family, 76
al-Yāzijī, Ibrāhīm, 75
al-Yāzijī, Ilyās, 66n
al-Yāzijī, Nāṣīf, 71 & n, 75-76
al-Yāzijī, Ni'mah, 66n
al-Yāzijī, Yūsuf, 66n

Ẓāhir al-'Umar, 50 & n, 61n, 64, 67 & n
Zaḥlah, 60 & n, 77
al-Za'īm, Būlus, *see* Paul of Aleppo
al-Za'īm, Cyril, *see* Cyril al-Za'īm
al-Za'īm, Ḥusnī, 93
al-Za'īm, Macarius, *see* Macarius al-Za'īm
al-Za'īm, Meletius, *see* Macarius al-Za'īm
Zākhir, 'Abdallāh, 52, 56n, 60
Zaydān, Jurjī, 88 & n
Zionist, 94